KU-765-093

Powerful Writing Skills

A quick and handy guide for any
manager or business owner

Written by Richard Andersen

CAREER PRESS
180 Fifth Avenue
P.O. Box 34
Hawthorne, NJ 07507
1-800-CAREER-1
201-427-0229 (outside U.S.)
FAX: 201-427-2037

POWERFUL WRITING SKILLS
A QUICK AND HANDY GUIDE FOR ANY MANAGER OR BUSINESS OWNER
ISBN 1-56414-145-4, $8.95
Cover design by Digital Perspectives
Printed in the U.S.A. by Book-mart Press

To order this title by mail, please include price as noted above, $2.50 handling per order, and $1.00 for each book ordered. Send to: Career Press, Inc., 180 Fifth Ave., P.O. Box 34, Hawthorne, NJ 07507

Or call toll-free 1-800-CAREER-1 (Canada: 201-427-0229) to order using VISA or MasterCard, or for further information on books from Career Press.

Library of Congress Cataloging-in-Publication Data

Powerful writing skills : a quick and handy guide for any manager or business
    owner.
       p.   cm. -- (Business desk reference)
    Includes index.
    ISBN 1-56414-145-4 $8.95
    1. Business writing. 2. English language--Business English.
I. Career Press Inc. II. Series.
HF5718.3.P685   1994
808'.06665--dc20   94-3751
                                                     CIP

Contents

National Press Publications, the product and publishing division of National Seminars Group, originally published this book for the training industry. Now this title is available exclusively to the trade from Career Press. Packed with real-world strategies and hands-on techniques, this resource is guaranteed to help you meet the career and personal challenges you face every day.

National Seminars Group, a division of Rockhurst College Continuing Education Center, Inc., has trained more than 2 million people in every imaginable occupation to be more productive and advance their careers. Along the way, they've learned what it takes to be successful, how to build the skills to make it happen and how to translate learning into results.

1
Make Your Words Talk

"Man does not live by words alone, but he sometimes has to eat them."
—Adlai Stevenson

Everything you write is a chance to make a good impression. If your writing contains mistakes, your readers will think you are careless or illiterate. If it is filled with jargon, your readers will think you are lazy or incapable of saying what you mean. If what you write is not easy to read, your readers will think your mind is not clear about what you say. Clear writing is the sign of a clear mind, and those who capture their ideas on paper stand out as fluent, confident and persuasive.

Think differently about yourself

Few things improve writing as much as a change in attitude. Think of yourself as a writer. Regardless of the kind of work you do, you are a writer. Your job is to communicate information and inspire people to act.

However, don't be a writer with a capital "W," the kind that knows everything there is to know about writing except how to enjoy it. In other words, take your subject seriously but take yourself with a grain of salt. If you don't, your tone will sound hollow, your sentences will attract mold and your reader's mind will blur with all of the "of's" and "which's" you've used.

Care about the economy and beauty of clear, straightforward prose. Try not to lose your personality in the monotone of what you've been taught to admire as "professional." Consider this example of what many people consider good professional writing:

> The general problem is perhaps correctly stated as the inadequacy of nursing personnel to understand the demands of nursing services. Inadequacy is both a quantitative and a qualitative term and can indicate the insufficient numbers of nursing personnel recruited to meet the demands for service.

What's the writer saying? Could you understand these two sentences after reading them once? Wouldn't it have been clearer if you had been told that there just aren't enough good nurses to go around? If you had to read that paragraph twice, so would most readers. Chances are you didn't even read it once; you just skimmed your way through to what you're reading now. If your writing is similar to that of the example paragraph, your readers will respond the same way you did. That means you'll spend time correcting the mistakes that come from their not having read your message, or you'll be on the phone answering questions about what you meant to say. Either way, you've lost time and energy that could have been devoted to other tasks.

Think differently about your readers

The trouble with most business memos and letters is that they stick too close to the same standard: "In reference to your letter of ...," "Enclosed herewith ...," "Pursuant to our telephone conversation ..." Who are these people who say the same words over and over again? Don't they have personalities that should reflect themselves in our language?

Writing is communication. When your writing fails to meet your readers' needs, you've failed to communicate. A clear sense of whom you are writing to is critical for successful communication. Organize and present your ideas with a targeted reader in mind. Don't be satisfied with putting down data and results or observations and opinions. Find a way to make this information meaningful to your reader.

This doesn't mean that you should talk down to your readers, however. When you lower yourself to what you think might be your readers' level, you actually insult them. You think you're being humble, but you may come across as arrogant.

Think of your readers as being just as intelligent and sincere about their jobs as you are. Even if they aren't, they'll appreciate you assuming they are. Respect for your readers goes a long way toward helping them see you as intelligent, reasonable and well-informed. Try to imagine what they might ask you, what they might object to, what they might already know and what they might find interesting.

Think differently about your subject

Show enthusiasm for your message. Studies show that readers respond positively to memos and letters that contain a sense of the writer's enthusiasm. They're encouraged to feel the time they spend reading the message is worthwhile.

This doesn't mean that you should announce your excitement. Let the subject speak for itself, but choose words that convey your sense of enthusiasm. Expressions such as "without equal," "the most important factor" and "strongly recommend" show the reader that you're moved by the significance of your subject.

Writing for Style

"I never write 'metropolis' for seven cents because I can get the same price for 'city.' I never write 'policeman' because I can get the same money for 'cop.'"

—Mark Twain

Your style is the way you say and do things. It makes you who you are, separates you from everyone else and identifies you as you. In the same way that you have your own particular way of speaking and acting, you also have your own writing style. Or you should have.

Unfortunately, most of us don't know what our individual writing styles are because we were never given the opportunities to discover them. Instead, we were taught to imitate other people's styles. First our teachers' and later our bosses' styles.

To help you write in the same voice you would use when you speak, consider the following suggestions:

1. Don't write any word that you wouldn't say. "Perusal," "Pursuant to" and "As per your request" are examples of this kind of writing.

2. Don't substitute the impersonal "one" for "you," "we" or "I." When we speak, we rarely say "one must" or "one should"; we say "I must" and "you should."

3. Use contractions. Because we often speak in contractions, they are a subtle way to draw readers into our messages and present ourselves as warm, accessible, friendly human beings.

Now this doesn't mean you should write *exactly* like you talk. Remember that you have many different speaking voices. You speak one way to your children and another way to your parents; one way to your bosses and another way *about* your bosses. If you're writing to a colleague, write in the voice you would use when speaking to that colleague. When writing to a boss or supervisor, write in the voice you would use when speaking to that boss or supervisor. This way, you'll always write in your own natural writing voice, yet maintain the professional tone or standard level of English that your memos and letters are expected to have.

Editing for Style

"I may be the world's worst writer, but I'm the world's best rewriter."
—James Michener

Good writers know that writing in their own voices only sounds good. The best writing comes from rewriting, and good writers spend more time rewriting than anything else. Their goal is to create carefully constructed prose that never loses the illusion of natural speech.

By writing frequently in your natural speaking voice, you will develop your own writing style. By rewriting what you write, you will retain the energy and power of your natural voice with all the hems, haws and digressions cut out.

After you've finished writing a memo or letter, ask yourself these questions:

Is it easy to understand? Does it say what I want it to say in a simple, clear and straightforward way?

Does it get to the point? Most of the time, the sooner we get to the point, the better.

Does it stick to the point? Does the memo or letter remain faithful to my stated purpose? Have I kept the reader's needs continually in view? Are all my points clearly illustrated?

Is it organized in a logical way? Does my opening sentence focus the reader's attention in the directions I want him or her to go? Does each sentence build in some way on the one that came before it? Are there any illogical surprises? Does material need to be added, moved or omitted? To begin answering these questions, proofread your memo or letter from the reader's point of view. Ask yourself, "What's in this for the reader? Why should the reader agree with me?"

Does it contain any unnecessary words? The more words we can eliminate from our writing, the more power we preserve. Consider how many words the writer of the following paragraph uses to tell people to start showing up on time for work:

> It has been recently brought to our attention that many people are beginning to show up past designated arrival times. This is not pursuant to company policy. Try to leave yourself enough time when you leave your homes in the morning to reach work by the arrival times that the personnel department has established as appropriate for your division.

Is it complete? Does it contain all the information the reader *needs* to know? Not every reader needs to know all the information that exists on any one subject.

Is it positive? Many times we disagree not with the opinion but with the way it is presented. Try not to be patronizing or condescending to your reader. See if you can present the negative in a positive or at least a neutral light. Instead of focusing on what your company rejects, emphasize what it approves of. Studies show that readers respond better to "Be on time" than "Don't be late." "We are unable to use your proposal" doesn't hit the reader with nearly the same force as "We are not going to use your proposal." Which would you rather be told: "Your letter reads easily, but there are several things you failed to include" or "Your letter reads easily, and here are a couple of things you can do to make your next letter even more effective"?

Is it accurate? Have you exaggerated anything, been unfair in any way or failed to distinguish between fact and interpretation? If you do anything to break your reader's trust, your reader will never trust you again.

Does it flow? Is it easy to read even if the subject is complex? Does the information get in the way of understanding? The more complicated the information, the shorter the sentences should be.

Does the opening grab my attention? If you don't have your readers' attention in the first five to 10 seconds, their attention will drift. To grab your readers' attention and make them want to continue:

1. **Make a point up front.** Tell the reader what your message is about in the opening line.

2. **State the good news.** Tell the reader what he or she wants to hear most. Put what benefits the reader right at the beginning.

3. **Ask a question.** When your reader answers it, he or she will be participating in your letter right from the start.

4. **Present a gripping fact.** Don't just state information; present it in a way that's meaningful to the reader. Compare "Earnings were down .7% in the last quarter" with "If we don't start making a profit soon, the photocopy machine will have to be monitored, outside telephone lines will have to be restricted and those in sales will have to pay for their own postage."

Is it correct? Although words and the ways they are used can change, most standards of meaning and usage remain the same. Even if your writing is clear, logical, precise and attention-grabbing, you will undermine your credibility with the reader if your choice of words is not consistently correct and appropriate.

Consider, for example, the word "boss." Dictionaries define "boss" as an employer or supervisor of workers. Given this definition, it is correct to refer to a supervisor as a "boss." Given the negative connotations often associated with the word, however, "boss" rarely appears in business writing. The definition may be correct, but in this context the word is inappropriate.

Make mistakes such as this and your readers will think you are either careless or uneducated. They will respond the same way for errors in spelling, punctuation and grammar. Try to make everything you write as close to perfect as you can.

4
Paragraphs

"When I see a paragraph shrinking under my eyes like a strip of bacon, I know I'm on the right track."

—Peter DeVries

Paragraphs are like rest stops. They give our eyes and mind a break. They tell us we've just come to the end of something and can take a breath before going on to the next matter.

In grammar school, we were taught that every paragraph has to have a beginning, a middle and an end. Today, paragraphs can be any length. They can be as short as one sentence or even one word. One-word paragraphs make very powerful paragraphs.

Right?

Instead of thinking of paragraphs as having beginnings, middles and ends, consider good paragraphs as having:

Unity. Try to stick to one idea in each paragraph and place that idea in the opening sentence. This lets your reader know what your paragraph is about and the attitude he or she should have toward your subject. The concluding sentence of your paragraph should lead your reader into the opening sentence of the paragraph that follows.

Coherence. "Coherence" comes from the Latin word meaning "to stick together." Paragraph coherence means that the sentences in the paragraph connect.

Each is in some way tied to the one that came before it. To create coherent paragraphs:

1. **Arrange the sentences in a logical pattern or order.** The order may be one of time, space, size, importance, general to specific or similarity and difference.

2. **Keep a consistent point of view.** Avoid shifting from one person to another, from one tense to another or from singular to plural without good reason. Consider beginning a new paragraph for every shift in person, tense and number.

3. **Repeat key words or phrases.** Or use synonyms. This keeps the readers' attention focused from one idea to the next.

4. **Use transitional words or phrases.** Transitional words help the reader get from one idea to the next.

   - Words that indicate addition include: again, also, and, and then, besides, further, furthermore, moreover, in addition.

   - Words that indicate order are: first, second, third, next, finally.

   - Words that indicate summary are: in brief, in short, in conclusion.

   - Words that indicate example are: for example, for instance, in particular.

   - Words that indicate result are: as a result, consequently, therefore, then, thus, so, for this reason.

- Words that indicate comparison include: similarly, in the same way as, more than, less than.

- Words that indicate contrast include: however, nevertheless, on the other hand, yet, unlike, but, despite, in spite of.

- Words that indicate time include: afterward, immediately, meanwhile, soon, now, at last, presently, shortly.

Emphasis. Begin and end each paragraph with important pieces of information and well-written sentences. This will make your reader want to continue from one paragraph to the next.

Here are some examples of the kinds of opening sentences that help maintain a reader's attention:

- **Name the person or audience you are addressing.** This almost always catches the reader's attention and directs him or her to the words that follow.

- **Begin with an answer to a question or opposing point of view** that may be raised in the reader's mind by something you said in your previous paragraph.

- **State the main idea of the paragraph in the opening sentence.** Follow with the reason why it should or should not be supported.

- **Ask a question.** When the reader answers it, he or she is involved in your subject.

- **Make a prediction.** You can point to the consequences of a present situation by telling your reader what will happen if he or she doesn't act now.

- **Open with an appealing or amusing incident** that will arouse your reader's curiosity.

The closing sentence of each paragraph is the best place to form a link with the opening sentence of the next paragraph, but ask yourself in you need one. If each paragraph in your memo or letter develops a point in a series, you don't need to sum up what you've said before going on to the next paragraph. Unless the information is so important it merits repetition, end each paragraph with a transition that makes the reader want to hurry on to the next paragraph.

Here are some of the kinds of endings you can close your paragraphs with:

- Summarize the main point of the paragraph and introduce the reader to the point that will begin the next paragraph.

- Restate the paragraph's thesis if it was about something you hoped to prove.

- Direct the reader's attention to the possible consequences of a situation already presented in the paragraph.

- Call upon the reader to act or tell the reader what action you will take.

- End with a quotation that confirms the views presented in the paragraph.

The last line of the last paragraph of any memo or letter is almost as important as the opening one. Well-written endings give readers a sense of completeness.

Their interest, which was aroused in the opening line and maintained in the opening lines or the subsequent paragraphs, should be satisfied in the concluding line of the last paragraph.

To prevent disappointing your readers:

1. Do not introduce a new idea into the concluding line of your memo or letter. If it is important, incorporate it into the main body of what you've written.

2. Do not begin you last sentence with "In conclusion" or "To summarize." Well-written endings are self-evident.

3. Do not apologize for your opinions. You're entitled to them, and if they are substantially supported and carefully presented, they won't require an admission of whatever inadequacies you might feel.

A final word about paragraphs

Use indented paragraphs. Our eyes are accustomed to them. Since we learned to read, school books, magazines, newspapers and novels have shown us only indented paragraphs. Our eyes have been trained to recognize each new indented paragraph as a chunk of new information to process. If blocks of type are used, the beginning of a new paragraph may not be noticed, especially if it begins at the top of a page or below an illustration or table.

The reason why we often find block paragraphs in business correspondence is because early typewriters didn't have tabs, and today, some people follow the old

style. There isn't much of a reason to use block paragraphs, and with modern typewriters and word processing systems, we can eliminate them completely.

Construct your paragraphs with a good eye as well
as a good mind. Enormous blocks of print implant the
image of a difficult subject in your reader's minds.
Breaking a long paragraph in two, even if it isn't necessary, can be an important visual aid. On the other hand,
a whole bunch of short paragraphs one right after the
other can be distracting. The safest policy is to vary the
length of your paragraphs without making the breaks
seem forced or unnatural. Few things irritate readers
more than picking up an attractive page of prose only to
have sentences pulled out from under them when they
least expect it.

Consider how the paragraph you just read looks on
the page. Would it be more appealing to the eye to divide it into two paragraphs, with the second paragraph
beginning "The safest policy is..."?

Now consider the above divided this way:

Construct your paragraphs with a good eye as well
as a good mind.

Enormous blocks of print implant the image of a difficulty subject in your readers' minds. Breaking a long
paragraph into two, even if it isn't necessary, can be an
important visual aid.

On the other hand, a whole bunch of short paragraphs can be distracting.

The safest policy is to vary the length of your paragraphs without making the breaks seemed forced or unnatural.

Few things irritate readers more than picking up an
attractive page of prose only to have sentences pulled
out from under them when they least expect it.

Obviously, no rule governs the length of paragraphs. A paragraph should be as long as or as short as is necessary to cover the idea presented in the paragraph. Generally speaking, however, the shorter the paragraphs and the fewer the number of ideas contained in them, the easier they are to read.

5

Sentences

> *"A sentence should contain no unnecessary words, a paragraph no unnecessary sentences, for the same reason that a drawing should have no unnecessary lines and a machine no unnecessary parts. This requires not that the writer make all his sentences short, or that he avoid all detail and treat his subjects only in outline, but that every word tell."*
> —Strunk, W. and White, E.B.: *The Elements of Style,* New York, Macmillan Co, 1959, p ix.

The most effective way to write lively, powerful, engaging sentences is to write as close as possible to the way you speak. In other words, be yourself. Once you have the energy of clear, honest, natural words on paper, then you can forge them into the kinds of sentences that Ernest Hemingway says separate architecture from interior decorating. Here are some tips on how to do it:

Choose nouns over adjectives. Adjectives are indispensable to speech, but there isn't one that can replace even the weakest noun. Nouns are where the information is. They're the names of the people, places and things that our readers want most to know about.

Adjectives drain most nouns of their color. Especially if they are overdone. The adjective "very," for example, is particularly debilitating: "This is a very important lesson that we should all pay very close attention to."

Choose verbs over adverbs. Verbs are where the action is. They're the ones that give good writing its power. Although there is nothing wrong with adverbs, you preserve energy in a sentence every time you eliminate one or replace it and the verb it assists with a stronger verb. Consider the difference between "John went quickly to the photocopy machine" and "John rushed to the photocopy machine." The word "rushed" is doing more than twice the work of "went" and "quickly."

Choose plain words over fancy ones. Let your ear be your guide. If you wouldn't say the word, you're probably better off not writing it. Rich, ornate, beauteous words are often unhealthy and sometimes sickening.

Choose specific words over general ones. One of the surest ways to hold any reader's attention is to be specific. The more specific you are, the sharper the pictures you create in the readers' minds, and the better they remember what you've said. Instead of telling your reader, "I'll call you next week about this problem," consider, "Joan, I'll call you next Thursday afternoon about Bob's request for a raise. Let me know then what you want me to tell him." "I'll call you next week" is too vague. "I'll call you next Thursday afternoon," however, lets Joan know that Thursday afternoon she's going to hear from you. During the week, she's going to be thinking about that telephone call, and chances are good that when you call she'll have some idea of what she wants you to tell Bob.

Choose short sentences over long sentences. Especially if the information is complicated. Some editors claim that any sentence with more than 17 words is too long, but there is no sure-fire rule governing the length of sentences. A sentence should be as short or as long as necessary to express a complete thought. Generally speaking, short sentences are easier to read. However, beware of lining up too many short sentences in a row:

> I received your order for 25 office chairs on October 4. A labor strike has delayed shipment. We recently hired new workers. Your chairs will be on their way in a week. I apologize for the inconvenience. It won't happen again. Your patience is appreciated.

Choose the personal over the impersonal. People enjoy reading and responding to other people. Instead of merely stating the benefits of a particular product, service or idea, show the reader how what you have to offer will benefit him or her in personal way. Say, for example, you want your client to renew his insurance policy. Instead of just pointing out how much money your client will be awarded under what circumstances, remind your client of the time he or she had an accident and how quickly your company responded. Or tell your client about the time something happened to another client and how you were able to help that person in ways other insurance companies couldn't.

A final word about sentences

Draw a slash through each period in every memo or letter you write. If the distance between slashes is approximately the same, all your sentences are pretty much the same length; and if all of your sentences are approximately the same length, you're putting your reader to sleep. Vary the length of your sentences the same way you would vary the length of your paragraphs: it is a subtle way to keep your reader awake.

6

Phrases

"Style is the effectiveness of assertion."
—George Bernard Shaw

A phrase is a group of words that doesn't have a subject or a verb but gives meaning to a sentence:

The insurance agent runs his business *from a computer in his living room.*

One of the first signs of insecure writers is the number of phrases they use to say what could be said in just a few words. Instead of writing "now" or "then", these writers use "at this point in time." Not only do these phrases pad messages with unnecessary words, but we've heard them before. Many times before.

Clichés

Phrases that unnecessarily lengthen messages and have been repeated so often as to become clichés work against us in two ways: they bore the reader and dehumanize the writer by using artificial voices.

Nevertheless, we continue to put these prefabricated phrases into our memos and letters because we've learned to depend on them. Phrases such as "In reference to your letter of ...," "As per our telephone conversation of ...," and "Enclosed herewith please find ...," help us get started. Once we have these words down on paper, we've been given the momentum to add whatever other words are necessary to complete the opening paragraph. Then we search our stock of clichés for a way to open the second paragraph. The final line of our memos and letters ends with "If you have any questions, please do not hesitate to contact me."

Sound familiar? These phrases may help us begin paragraphs and end letters, but they also undermine whatever power our subject may have by numbing the reader's senses.

Use these phrases if you need them to get started. Then, once you've completed your memo or letter, go back and see how many of them you can eliminate. If you feel you need the information contained in the prefabricated phrase, see if you can reword it. Instead of saying, "Pursuant to our agreement," for example, try "When we agreed to ..."

Another problem with prefabricated phrases is that they are often too general or vague. That's why we can use them in so many different contexts. Unfortunately, they don't inspire our readers to act quickly or as efficiently as specific instructions. "I look forward to your response regarding this matter" is not nearly as effective as "Make sure those figures are on my desk by Tuesday at 10 o'clock."

Prepositional phrases

Having eliminated as many clichés such as "In reference to ..." and "In accordance with ..." as you can, look at your prepositional phrases. A prepositional phrase is a group of words introduced by a preposition. The preposition usually introduces a noun: "In the meeting room," "by the desk," or a pronoun: "to him," "for them." Most prepositional phrases are used as adjectives, "The subject of the article on sales techniques ...," or adverbs, "He went to New York to sign the contract."

Prepositional phrases become a problem when you line up too many in a row. Notice how quickly your reading energy is drained by the parade of prepositional phrases in the following sentence: "The Danubian Basin changed rapidly under the impact of forces within the core area of the rising economic system." Here's some advice for handling prepositional phrases:

Two prepositional phrases in a row: no problem.

Three in a row: think twice about it.

Four in a row: almost always a disaster.

If you write three or four consecutive prepositional phrases, see if you can spread the information they contain over several sentences. Or perhaps some of the information can be placed in another paragraph.

And speaking of prepositions...remember being told it's wrong to end a sentence with a preposition? Thanks to Winston Churchill, it's okay now to end a sentence with a preposition. Once asked if he ever ended a sentence with a preposition, Churchill replied, "Ending a sentence with a preposition is something up with which I will not put." He made us realize the absurdity of this rule. If when you speak you end your sentences in a preposition, it's also acceptable to end your sentences with a preposition when you write.

A final word on phrases

Phrases that have been around so long they've outlived their usefulness have no place in effective memos and letters. Allow the meaning of your message to choose your words rather than the other way around.

When you think of a specific person, place or thing, a picture comes into your mind. If you want to describe that person, place or thing, search for the words that best express what you see in your mind. In other words, don't search for words that will create a mental picture. See the picture first, then describe it.

When you begin your message with an abstract idea, you are more likely to have words in your mind rather than pictures. These words may hinder your developing a clear mental picture or change the meaning of what you want your readers to understand. It is probably better to avoid thinking of words until you can visualize what you want to say. This will help you see more clearly the stale or mixed images, the prefabricated phrases and the unnecessary repetitions. Then, if you're still not sure about the effect of a particular word or phrase, consult author George Orwell's guidelines for clear writing:

1. Never use a word or phrase that you are used to seeing in print.
2. Never use a phrase where a word will do.
3. If it's possible to cut a phrase, cut it.
4. Never use a foreign or scientific word or phrase if you can use an everyday English equivalent.

For additional advice on style, consult the following:

Associated Press Stylebook and Libel Manual. The Associated Press.

The Chicago Manual of Style. The University of Chicago Press.

Webster's Standard and American Style Manual. Merriam-Webster, Inc.

The McGraw-Hill Style Manual. McGraw-Hill Book Company.

The New York Times Manual of Style and Usage. Times Books.

7
Words

"The small words work best and the old small words work best of all."
—Winston Churchill

Business writing is often cold, stiff and impersonal; and many business writers favor language that is pompous, archaic, trite and more formal than ordinary business situations require. Some favor the passive voice ("It has been brought to our attention ...") over the active voice ("We just learned ..."), and begin too many of their sentences with "it" ("It has been decided ..." or "It appears ..."). If you write a sentence in the passive voice, try switching to the active voice. Can you see the improvement? If you begin a sentence with "it" and the "it" doesn't refer to something in the previous sentence, cross out the "it" and perhaps the two or three words that follow. See the difference it makes:

It has been recently brought to our attention that many people are showing up late for work.

Many people are showing up late for work.

The most effective words are the ones you say every day. When you speak on the phone or in person, you know the words that work and those that don't. You've already tested them. So why not put these proven words into your writing? Write the way you speak and your writing will be much more lively, powerful and engaging than if you write the way you think writing should sound.

Tone

Writing, like conversation, has tone. The tone of your writing and speaking voices expresses the attitude you have toward your subject. Tone can be personal or impersonal, formal or informal, positive or negative. The way in which you handle the tone of voice in your writing plays an important role in determining your reader's reaction to what you have to say.

Generally speaking, the more natural the tone of your writing voice, the more appealing your message will be. Consider the following two sentences:

It is to be observed that contracting for services provides the only means available to us to ensure timely compliance.

Unless we provide some of these services by contracting businesses outside our own, we won't finish the project on time.

The sentences have the same meaning and length, but the tone in each is different. The first sentence is pretentious, impersonal and difficult to read. The second is much closer to the way we speak.

Here are some expressions that sound artificial compared with improvements that sounds natural. Notice how the natural phrasings sound more sincere:

Allow me to express our appreciation for...
Thank you for your help.

We wish to acknowledge receipt of...
We have your...

With regard to your letter of...
You say in your letter that...

Think of the people you like to hear from. Aren't they the ones who let their personalities come through regardless of their profession? The same is true for you. Your readers want to hear from the warm, genuine person they spoke to on the phone or met for lunch. So express yourself in writing the same way you speak. The more you are you, the more willing your readers will be to listen and to agree with what you have to say.

Here are some guidelines to help you to get your message across without taking away anything from who you are:

Use short words. Long words slow the reader down. Look at the words on the left-hand side of each of the columns listed below. Compare how long it takes to say them with the speed of the words in the parentheses.

affirmative (yes)	anticipate (expect)
cooperate (help)	determine (find)
facilitate (make easy)	forward (send)
inasmuch as (since)	indicate (show)
personnel (people)	prior to (before)
pertaining to (about)	presently (now)
request (ask)	submit (give)
terminate (end)	transpire (happen)

Use words like the ones in the parentheses, and your readers will understand your messages faster, easier and with fewer chances of misinterpreting what you say.

Use orthodox spelling. Writing "nite" for "night", "thru" for "through", and "cuz" for "because" may be acceptable in a personal letter or in the name of a store trying to catch people's attention (Kopy Kat PhotoKopy), but it has no place in business letters or memos.

Use necessary words. Eliminate any word that does not contribute to your message. The more unnecessary words you can eliminate, the stronger and clearer your writing will be. Consider the following sentences:

1. According to statistical data received by this office, there is an increasing amount of investment on the part of government being made available for computer research.
2. The government is increasing its investment in computer research.

Both sentences convey the same meaning, but notice how much shorter and easier to read is the second. Here are some phrases and their concise alternatives:

at this point in time	now
for the purpose of	to
in the event that	if
due to the fact that	because
in the final analysis	finally
until such time as	until

Use personal words. Until recently, using words such as "I" and "we" was considered bad form in business writing. The common substitute was the word "one." Today, with business writers moving toward greater directness and simplicity in their style, "I" and "we" are not only acceptable, they're encouraged.

Notice the difference between the impersonal sentence that follows and the improved rewrite:

If there are any problems regarding the above-mentioned matter, please direct all inquiries to the customer relations office.

If you have any problems, please contact me.

On the other hand, you don't want to be too personal. Notice the difference between the overly informal sentence and the improved rewrite:

You've got to remember that the main thing about taking minutes is that you get them transcribed quickly.

Please transcribe the meeting notes as soon as possible.

Notice, however, that even the wordy first example is preferable to the impersonal, detached, machine-like tone we've come to admire in as "professional." The best professional writing is somewhere in between. It achieves a sense of balance between the personal and the impersonal, the formal and the informal.

Use contractions. Unless you want to maintain a strictly formal relationship with your reader, consider using contractions. Because contractions are spoken so naturally, they are a very subtle way to draw the reader into your message and allow you to come across as warm and personal.

Use words that people like to hear. Positive-sounding words help create a positive response. Compare the words people like to hear in the column on the left with those that turn people off:

achieve	blame
appreciate	complain
success	failure
you say	you claim
can	impossible
welcome	won't

Use speaking words. Many writers feel they have to dress up ordinary words when they write. They want to sound learned and important, but they wind up sounding obscure and affected.

If you like to use pretentious-sounding word constructions such as the ones in the left-hand column, consider substituting the plain, simple words listed on the right:

heretofore	before
to be in receipt of	have
enclosed please find	here is
commensurate with	equal to
termination	end

Use correct words. Words that mean what they say and say what they mean. Here are some commonly misused words and what you can do about them:

Affect, effect. "Affect" is a verb. It means "to change" or "to influence." "Effect" can be a verb or a noun. As a verb, it means "to cause"; as a noun, it means "a result."

Aggravate, irritate. To "aggravate" is "to add to" something that is already troublesome; to "irritate" is "to annoy."

All right, alright. "Alright" is not a word. You'd never write "alwrong," would you?

Allude, elude. You "allude" or "make reference to" a book; you "elude" or "run away from" someone who is chasing you.

Alot. An "alot" is a camel. One thing we don't need in the office is a lot of "alots."

Among, between. Use "among" when more than two are involved; use "between" when you are comparing two persons, places or things.

And/or. A shortcut that looks and reads bad and can lead to confusion or ambiguity. Avoid whenever possible.

Anybody, anyone. "Anybody" is written as one word when it refers to "any person." "Any body" as two words means "any corpse" or "any group." The same is true for "everybody," "nobody" and "somebody." "Anyone" means "anybody"; "any one" means "any single person" or "any single thing."

Assure, ensure, insure. To "assure" is "to speak confidently" about something; to "ensure" is "to make sure" or "to make certain"; to "insure" is "to protect something against loss or damage with an insurance policy."

Being. Not needed after "regard" in sentences such as "He was regarded as being the best." Preferred is "He was regarded as the best."

Can, may. "Can" means "able to"; "may" means "permit." "Can I leave work early?" means "Am I able to leave work early?" "Is all my work done?" "Are my legs strong enough to carry me out?" "May I leave work early?" means "May I have permission to go home early?"

Compare to, compare with. To "compare to" is to point out the similarities in different things; to "compare with" is to point out the differences between similar things. Life can be compared to a rat race; rat races can be compared with rush-hour traffic.

Couldn't care less, could care less. "Couldn't care less" means you care so little about something it would be impossible for you to care less. "Could care less" is an expression that comes from people not hearing the "n't" in "couldn't care less."

Data. Like "media" and "phenomena," "data" is plural. It refers to more than one fact or piece of evidence. Nevertheless, it is becoming popular to refer to it as singular. Your choice: "The data is misleading" or "The data are misleading."

Disability, handicap. A "disability" is a physical or emotional impairment; a "handicap" occurs when a person cannot overcome his or her disability. A person in a wheelchair is handicapped in certain situations; a person who has learned to overcome a reading disability is no longer handicapped.

Disinterested, uninterested. To be "disinterested" is to be impartial, fair or without prejudice; to be "uninterested" is to be not interested.

Farther, further. "Farther" has to do with distance: "I traveled farther than you." "Further" can be used to indicate distance, but it can also be used as a verb meaning "to promote" or "to advocate": "I plan to further your cause."

Finalize. Can mean either "to terminate" or "to put into final form." Avoid the word altogether. It's overused, pretentious and pseudo-technical; substitute "finish" or "complete."

Fewer, less. "Fewer" has to do with numbers; "less" has to do with quantity. Fewer sales representatives spoke at this year's conference. (To use less here would mean that the people were missing arms and legs.) People are smoking less and exercising more.

Gratuitous, gratuity. Gratuitous means "undeserved" or "unearned"; a gratuity is a "tip for services rendered."

Hopefully. "Hopefully" used to mean "with hope"; now it means "I hope," and it drives office grammarians into fits of rage and exasperation. They reason that if you write "Hopefully, you will write your proposal on time," you don't know if you hope to write it or you are writing in a hopeful frame of mind. These same people who crusade against the common use of "hopefully," however, see nothing wrong with saying, "Admittedly, hopefully is an obsession of mine."

I, me. When our parents heard us say sentences such as "Bob and me played baseball," they told us to say "Bob and I." Because we were told so often to say "Bob and I," we tend to use "I" any time we join it with someone else's name. What's the best way to tell when to use "I" or "me"? Read the sentence without the other person's name.

Imply, infer. They don't mean the same thing. To "imply" is to suggest or indicate without expressing exactly what you want to say: "He implied that we were going to get a raise." To "infer" is to reach a conclusion from the evidence at hand: "Based on what he said, we can infer that a raise will be coming."

Irregardless. No such word. The word we want is "regardless."

Its, it's. "Its" is the possessive form of the word "it." It means something belongs to the particular place or thing "it" stands for: "This computer is more expensive than most because its screen is so large and clear." "It's" is the contraction for "it is": "It's a large and clear screen."

-ize. So many good verbs end in "-ize," we don't need to add this tempting suffix to any more. Listen to what sounds natural (words in the column on the left) and what sounds pseudo-intellectual (words in the column on the right):

criticize	finalize
harmonize	prioritize
fraternize	departmentalize
fertilize	stylize

Like, as. Except as a term of affection, "like" has to do with comparison: "That was not like him." "As" can be used in comparisons, "The two were equally as efficient" or "He was as efficient as she," but it also appears as the introduction or heading of a list, "The program included such topics as: ...".

Plan ahead. Would you ever "plan behind"? Just "plan" is sufficient.

Reason is because, reason is that. "Reason is because" is considered redundant because both "reason" and "because" have to do with cause. "Reason is that" is the grammatically correct expression.

Secondly, thirdly. If you wouldn't say "firstly"—and you definitely shouldn't—stick to "first," "second" and "third."

Thanking you in advance. Unnecessary words. In all cases, the plain, simple, straightforward "thank you" is sufficient.

Try to, try and. To "try to" is "to attempt." "To try and" implies that two separate actions are taking place: the "try" and whatever verb comes after it.

Unique. Because "unique" means "without equal," there can be no degree of uniqueness, no "most unique" or "very unique."

Use active voice. Most of the time active voice is shorter, simpler, clearer, more direct and easier to understand than passive voice. Active voice moves readers along; passive voice slows them down.

Passive voice is the language of irresponsibility. Its purpose is to mislead, distort and disguise. Very rarely will a company announce in the active voice, "We made a mistake." Almost always, the company will state: "An error was found." Apparently, it was lying in the hall and somebody happened to trip over it.

There are reasons for using passive voice constructions. Most of the time, however, they are unnecessary.

Passive: *The street was crossed by the chicken.*

Active: *The chicken crossed the street.*

Active voice puts the chicken and the road where they belong.

To discover passive voice, look for the word: "By." If the word "by" has a verb in front of it, you may have written something in the passive voice. See if it sounds better to change it to active. Almost everything we say is in the active voice.

Be consistent. Maintain the same verb tense throughout each paragraph that you write. If you begin a paragraph in the present tense, stay in the present tense until you end the paragraph. Or if you want to switch tenses, begin a new paragraph with every tense change.

Avoid "headline" words. "Headline" words are words that newspaper editors have shortened for reasons of space. Many may be inappropriate outside of the newspaper. Here are some headline words and what you want to substitute for them:

GOP	Republican Party
GM	General Motors
America	United States
Russia	Soviet Union
UN	United Nations
quote	quotation
recap	recapitulate

Avoid clichés. Clichés are expressions that have been used so often they've lost whatever energy they might originally have had. Here are some clichés and words to consider using in their place:

tried and true	reliable
the bottom line	the deciding factor
don't hesitate to call	please call
few and far between	rare
in a nutshell	in short
at this point in time	now

Avoid euphemisms. Euphemisms are words and phrases meant to hide negative things. Some of them— "deceased" for "dead", for example—have their place, but most of them dull our style and serve no useful role in business writing.

Euphemism	Alternative
revenue enhancement	price increases
negative impact	bad effect
pre-owned	used
contrary to expectations	unexpected

Avoid jargon. Use technical language or words peculiar to a special business when these words meet the needs of a particular reader. The rest of the time, write in plain, non-technical, conversational prose. Compare this sentence about computers, "Companies are increasingly turning to capacity planning techniques to determine when future processing loads will exceed processing capability," with "We're planning for the day when our computers run out of room." Other jargon words include: utilization, prioritization, interface, market penetration, impact (as a verb), optimize, task (as a verb), facilitated, economy and measures.

Avoid redundancy. Redundant writers can't let any single word do its job. Just to make sure they don't miss the importance of the point they're trying to make, these writers find all kinds of ways to say everything twice. "Unanimous" becomes "completely unanimous." Here are some more commonly used redundancies and their corresponding sufficient meanings:

brief in duration	brief
during the year 1990	during 1990
resulting effect	effect
unresolved problem	problem
repeat the same	repeat
surplus left over	surplus
advance warning	warning
three-month period	three months

Redundancy doesn't help clarify meaning or enrich style. Nevertheless, the repetition of certain key words and phrases can reinforce important points and enhance eloquence:

> *The chief problem we face is increasing competition: competition from Japan, competition from Taiwan, competition from Korea and competition from Germany.*

Keep related words together. Badly placed words and phrases can cause confusion in a sentence. Keep the words that have to do with a subject apart from those that do not have to do with that subject. Note in the following examples what the writers meant to say and what they actually said:

> *In accordance with your instructions, I have sold my stock in the enclosed envelope.*

> *I have been in the office with this proposal for two weeks.*

> *The city's first sperm bank opened with semen samples from 18 men frozen in a stainless steel tank.*

Avoid acronyms, initials and abbreviations. Not everyone knows that SALT means Strategic Arms Limitation Talks. Write out the complete name the first time it is used and place the acronym, initials or abbreviations in parentheses following the name. Once you've given your readers their bearings, you can use the acronym or the movement that you are writing about: "The National Association for the Advancement of Colored People (NAACP) will elect a new president this year."

Avoid sexist language. Words that favor one gender over the other have no place in business or any other kind of writing. Such language occurs mostly with the third-person masculine pronouns ("he," "him," "himself," "his") and with job titles that have a built-in gender preference ("foreman," "chairman," "stewardess").

To avoid sexist pronouns, use the "he or she" construction ("Each manager must file his or her report.") or switch to the less awkward plural "they," "them," "their," "themselves" whenever possible ("All managers must file their reports."). Although still seen as incorrect by grammarians, the use of a plural "they" to refer to a singular subject is yet another option. Follow the guidelines and philosophy of your organization when determining which option is best. To avoid sexist job titles, change to forms that have no gender:

mailman	letter carrier
salesman	sales representative
policeman	police officer
newsman	journalist
fireman	firefighter
chairman	chairperson
spokesman	spokesperson

Change sexist words that aren't necessarily job titles:

mankind	people
manned	staffed
average man	average person
all men	all people

Don't forget to give men and women equal treatment:

men and ladies	men and women
man and wife	husband and wife
John Dow and Mary	John Dow and Mary Ward

If you still think "man" can stand for both men and women, consider this sentence:

Modern man no longer pampers himself during pregnancy. He works almost up until the day of delivery and is back at work within a few weeks of leaving the hospital.

Use a thesaurus. But only to remember words, not to discover new ones. If we use the thesaurus to find big words that we can put in the place of little words, we risk distorting what we mean to say. If you've written a word and know there's a better word but can't remember what it is, reach for a thesaurus. Otherwise, most of the words you need to be a lively, powerful, engaging writer are in your mind and heart.

Use a dictionary. To discover the meaning or correct spelling of a word, your most reliable source is a dictionary. The first definition listed is usually the preferred usage. Here is a list of commonly used dictionaries:

Webster's New World Dictionary, 3rd Edition. Simon and Schuster.

Random House College Dictionary. Random House.

American Heritage Dictionary. Houghton Mifflin.

A final word about words

Verbs. When we read, we tend to look mostly at nouns—the names of people, places and things—that's where the information is. But as writers, the words we want to focus on are the verbs—that's where the information is.

Here's one kind of verb you may want to take a second look at:

Forms of the verb "to be." There's nothing wrong with these verb forms. The problem is, they are the most popular verb forms in the English language, and they've lost some of their power as a result. If you've written five or six sentences in a row and all your verbs are linked with any of these six words: "am," "is," "are," "was," "were" or "been," see if you can replace a few of these constructions with different verbs or verb forms. A sentence such as "He is going to be here on Tuesday," for example, could be changed to "He arrives on Tuesday."

Adjectives. Because we live in an advertising age, we've learned not to pay attention to adjectives. We've learned to see through the illusion of advertising to the specific details underneath. The specific details about any subject—person, place, product, service or idea—are what grabs the strongest hold on our imaginations. Compare "The new computer has proven to be a cost-effective alternative to the old word processors" with "The RAM has cut our operating costs by 30%." Or "Management needs to be apprised of possibilities for entering international markets with new products" with "Twenty percent of the British clerical force lacks a computer-centered data base."

When you've finished the first draft of any writing, go back and circle adjectives you've used. After each adjective, ask yourself this question: "What do I mean by this word?" Take the first answer that comes to mind, cross out the adjective and put what you mean in its place.

If, however, you think the adjective accurately captures your feel for the subject, leave the adjective; but in the next sentence, give a specific example of what you mean. To say your boss has bad manners doesn't stir your reader's imagination nearly as much as saying your boss makes you baby-sit for his daughter, clean his aquarium and take his dirty clothes to the laundry.

8
Mechanics

"Nothing you write, if you hope to be good, will come out as you first hoped."
—Lillian Hellman

Business professionals expect your writing to be correct. No matter how brilliant your ideas or provocative your analyses, mechanical mistakes will undermine your credibility.

What is "correct" or "incorrect," however, is not the province of any one person or school of thought. It belongs to the people who speak the language. They create the rules and, because language is like life, the rules are not always consistent. The rules, like people, sometimes change and sometimes contradict each other. What's true in one situation doesn't hold up in another. Or what was true one year ago no longer applies now. It used to be you couldn't split an infinitive or end a sentence with a preposition. Now you can. Many well-educated, accomplished writers begin their sentences with "And" or "But," and follow the singular "none" with a plural verb ("None of you are wrong").

Because language is constantly changing, it's conceivable that in the not too distant future, it will be acceptable to not distinguish between "who" and "whom," substitute "like" for "as" and comma splice as many sentences as desired.

But what about today? How can you get a handle on what's acceptable in a business memo or letter and what isn't? How can you resolve the conflict between what is "correct" and what is "incorrect"?

Be yourself. The closer you write to the way you speak, the more powerful, lively, engaging and "correct" your writing will be. You speak in simple, clear, easy to understand sentences. These sentences are easy to construct and punctuate. Compare the sentence below with what follows it:

The Privacy Act of 1974 provides that each federal agency inform individuals, whom it asks to supply information, of the authority for the solicitation of the information and whether disclosure of such information is mandatory or voluntary; the principle purpose or purposes for which the information is to be used; the routine uses which may be made of the information; and the effects on the individual of not providing the information.

The Privacy Act of 1974 says that each federal agency that asks you for information must tell you whether the law says you have to give it, what the agency wants the information for and what will happen to you if you do not give it.

Because the first sentence is written like the writer thinks a message like this should sound, the chance of misinterpretation is greatly increased. The second sentence, though also long, is easier to read and much easier to punctuate.

Assume a new identity. After you've finished being yourself on paper, become a copyeditor. You want to see what you said, not what you wanted to say. The best way to do this is to:

1. Sit back and relax.
2. Read your memo or letter several times.
3. Allow your mistakes to emerge naturally from the page.

If you find some mistakes still slipping through:

1. Put a blank piece of paper over all the lines of your memo or letter except the last.
2. Read the last line backwards.
3. Move the paper up one line and read backwards the second line from the last.
4. Do this for the entire memo or letter.

This will help you discover misspelled words and typographical errors. Then reverse the process. Start with the first line and work your way down through the memo or letter. You'll discover the times you write "their" for "there" or "too" for "to." If you come across a phrase or sentence that you're not sure is correct, read it out loud. Your ears will tell you. If the sentence sounds right, it probably is, even if it doesn't conform to someone else's idea of what's right and wrong.

Nevertheless, we want to be correct. Consult your company's policy regarding business correspondence or one of the following guides:

Booher, Dianna. *Good Grief/Good Grammar*. New York. NY: Facts on File.

Boston, Bruce. *Stet: Tricks of the Trade for Writers and Editors*. Alexandria, VA: Editorial Experts, Inc.

Brandretti, Gyles. *The Joy of Lex*. New York, NY: William Morrow and Co.

Eschholz, Paul, Rosa, Alfred and Clark, Virginia. *Language Awareness*. New York, NY: St. Martin's Press.

Higgins, John. Sixth Edition: *English Simplified*. Grand Rapids, MI: Harper & Row Publishing.

Maggio, Rosalie. *The Nonsexist Word Finder: A Dictionary of Gender-Free Usage*. Boston, MA: Beacon Press.

Pinckert, Robert. *Pinckert's Practical Grammar*. Cincinnati, OH: Writer's Digest Books.

Shertzer, Margaret. *The Elements of Grammar*. New York, NY: Macmillan Publishing Co.

Smith, Peggy. *Simplified Proofreading*. Alexandria, VA: Editorial Experts, Inc.

Smith, Peggy. *Mark My Words: Instruction and Practice in Proofreading*. Alexandria, VA: Editorial Experts, Inc.

Strunk, William and White, E.B. *The Elements of Style*. New York, NY: Macmillan Publishing Co.

Warriner, John E. *English Composition and Grammar—Third Course*. San Diego, CA: Harcourt, Brace, Jovanovich, Publishing.

9

Spelling

"It's a damn poor mind that can think of only one way to spell a word."

—Andrew Jackson

If you're a poor speller, you'll probably always be a poor speller. Spelling is not a sign of intelligence; it's a question of brain function. Some people have it and some don't—the same way some people are more suited to math and others are more suited to literature. Nevertheless, there are a few things you can do to cut down on your spelling mistakes:

Stick to the words you say. Ninety percent of all good writing consists of only a thousand words. These thousand words are the same words we say every day. Studies show that we know how to spell practically all of the words we say. In fact, we don't say many words we don't know how to spell. If, when you write, you only use words that you say, you're going to cut down on your spelling mistakes. Following is a list of the kinds of words we tend to say and the kind we tend to write. Notice how much more difficult to spell are the ones we tend to write:

Words we say	Words we write
make easy	facilitate
trouble	inconvenience
about	pertaining to
home	residence

show	reveal
later	subsequent
enough	sufficient
happen	transpire
stop	terminate

Pronounce words carefully. If you pronounce them correctly, you'll probably spell them correctly:

library	surprise
accidentally	February

Watch for words that sound alike.

accept-except	vain-vein
altar-alter	here-hear
passed-past	it's-its

Watch for words that look alike.

loose-lose	quite-quit
choose-chose	moral-morale
proceed-precede	personal-personnel

Look for prefixes. Few people have trouble spelling the everyday words learned as children ("eye," "thought," "one") regardless of how difficult the spelling or the pronunciation. The words that cause the most spelling trouble are the ones we learned from reading. Many of these came from other languages, especially Latin, and most consist of three parts: a prefix, a base to which prefixes and suffixes are attached and a suffix.

Spelling words with prefixes is difficult because we don't use the words very often, we don't recognize the prefix as a prefix and the same prefix may be spelled in different ways for different words.

Fortunately, we know enough prefix-stem-suffix constructions that we don't have to be Latin scholars to understand them. Nevertheless, we can improve our spelling ability—and develop our vocabularies—by breaking words down into parts. Say, for example, we know the meaning of the prefix "uni-": "one" or "single." And say we know the word "uniform." Then we come across a word we might not know: "unilateral." Knowing the prefix helps us determine the meaning.

Guidelines for prefixes

Although there are numerous inconsistencies in spelling words with prefixes, there are a few rules that hold true in most cases:

The spelling of the base or root of a word is never changed by the addition of a prefix.

mis + spell = misspell
trans + plant = transplant
un + necessary = unnecessary
a + rouse = arouse

Many prefixes also keep the same form, regardless of the base or root to which they are attached.

dis/appear	for/bid
dis/appoint	for/sake
dis/satisfied	for/swear

Some prefixes change their last letter to fit better with the words they are attached to.

ad/mit	en/grave
ad/junct	en/ter
ag/gression	em/power

Some prefixes (and these are the most troublesome) are similar in sound but are spelled differently.

ante (meaning before); antedate, antecedent
anti (meaning against); anticlimax, antibody

inter (meaning between); interpret, interrupt
intra (meaning within); intramural, intravenous

Watch for suffixes. If the root word ends with an "e," and the first letter of the ending you want to add begins with a vowel ("a," "e," "i," "o," "u" or "y"), drop the "e" before adding your ending:

> arrang(e)ing
> com(e)ing
> combin(e)ation

If your ending doesn't begin with a vowel, keep the "e."

> careful
> entirely
> placement

Two exceptions: If the root word ends with a vowel ("a," "e," "i," "o," "u" or "y") and the letter before the vowel is a "c" or a "g," keep the vowel if you're adding an ending that begins with an "a" or an "o."

> noticeable
> changeable
> manageable

Notice how other people spell. Not just the words you have trouble with but new ones as well.

Books, magazines, newspapers, even restaurant menus can help. Consider reading with a pen—underline the correct spelling of the words you have trouble with, list them on a piece of paper and tape them to your bulletin board or the inside of your desk drawer. That way you don't have to look them up every time you want to use them.

Many words have two or more acceptable spellings. This is especially true of words that come from languages that do not use the Latin alphabet. "Usable," for example, can also be spelled "useable." The first spelling that appears in your dictionary is the most common. Unless your company suggests otherwise, use the most common spelling. Here is a short list of words that can be spelled more than one way.

sulfur/sulphur	luster/lustre
combating/combatting	theater/theatre
labeled/labelled	caliph/kalif

10

Punctuation

"Those who write clearly have readers; those who write obscurely have commentators."
—Albert Camus

Punctuation marks are like traffic signals. They direct readers where you want them to go. A period (.) means to come to a full stop, a semicolon (;) means to stop and proceed, a comma (,) means to slow down and the absence of any punctuation means to keep going. Writers and readers, like drivers, move smoothly when they obey the signs. Look at the difference a comma makes in the following sentences:

Let's talk turkey.

Let's talk, turkey.

Although there are many rules governing punctuation, they don't solve all punctuation problems. Decisions about whether or where to use a particular punctuation mark often involve questions of style and emphasis—issues that cannot always be reduced to a designated set of rules. Like style, punctuation is something of an art and, like art, it can be developed through the use and practice of certain skills. Punctuation marks are the tools writers use to make their art more accessible to the reader.

In this book, punctuation problems are covered selectively, that is, with an emphasis on correcting the errors that appear most frequently in business writing.

The comma

A comma and a conjunction join two sentences:

The report has been issued, and its recommendations have been accepted.

The new photocopy machine will save us time, but we have to walk over to another building to get to it.

A comma separates an introduction from the main part of a sentence:

Because Dr. Jones will be lecturing in London this week, Wednesday's meeting has been canceled.

On the other hand, our profits were much higher than we expected.

A comma separates information that isn't part of the main sentence:

National Seminars, located in Kansas City, offers a wide range of courses.

The program, because it wasn't carefully thought out, was difficult to maintain.

A comma separates elements in a simple series.

The flag is red, white and blue.

Notice the absence of the comma before the conjunction "and." Problems can occur, however, in a complex sentence where the absence of the comma confuses the reader. For example:

Mary's areas of study are the Harlem Renaissance, Contemporary Women Writers and Feminist Literary Criticism.

Is Mary studying two or three areas? Therefore, don't include the comma in a simple series; include the comma when leaving it out might cause confusion.

Commas identify quotations:

Mark Twain tells us, "There are two times in a man's life when he should not speculate: when he can't afford it and when he can."

"The business of America," said Calvin Coolidge, "is business."

"Lobbyists are the touts of protected industries," Winston Churchill told the press.

Commas separate words from those they are sometimes connected with:

Los Angeles, California, is the home of the Dodgers; Anaheim, California, is the home of the Angels. The way the people drive there, you are either one or the other.

There are, however, some exceptions to this rule: Sr., Jr., Ph.D., M.D., D.Ed., Inc., Ltd., and esq.—though you wouldn't be wrong if you left the comma in. Both of the following are correct:

Andrew Rabinowitz, M.D. is giving the lecture.

Andrew Rabinowitz, M.D., is giving the lecture.

The most important thing to remember is consistency. Establish which is your organization's preferred usage and be consistent.

When the title is part of a name, eliminate all the commas. You'd never write "Earl, the Pearl," for example. "Earl the Pearl and Dean the Dream were Knicks."

The comma splice

The comma splice is two independent sentences joined incorrectly with a comma.

"Mary mailed the envelope, John received the letter."

To make the sentences correct, you could replace the comma with a semicolon:

"Mary mailed the envelope; John received the letter."

Another option is to separate the two independent thoughts into two sentences. Yet a third possibility is to use a comma and a coordinating conjunction.

"Mary mailed the envelope, and John received the letter."

To determine whether you want to separate your sentences with a period, a semicolon or a comma and a conjunction, read them out loud. Each solution will give your sentences a slightly different tone or meaning. By reading them out loud, you can also best determine the most effective structure. The most appropriate structure, however, will probably be your company's policy regarding comma splices.

The colon

Use the colon to announce an important statement, a list of items or a long quotation.

Corporation: an ingenious device for obtaining individual profit without individual responsibility.

There are three kinds of salespeople: those who are winners and know they are winners, those who are losers and know they are losers and those who are winners but don't know it. The last are the most dangerous. They never give up trying.

Ron Luciano tells us: "When I started as an umpire, baseball was played by nine tough competitors on grass in graceful ballparks. By the time I retired, there were ten men on each side, the game was played indoors on plastic and I had to spend half of my time watching out for a man dressed in a chicken suit who kept trying to kiss me."

The semicolon

When there were only the period and the comma, there were only two rules: if you want a long pause between two thoughts, put in a period; if you want a short pause, put in a comma. The semicolon was invented to create a longer pause than a comma and a shorter pause than a period. Since then it has become one of the most hated punctuation marks. Most writers don't use it.

The most common use for the semicolon today is to join two sentences. The semicolon enables the sentence to move a little more quickly than if a period separated the two sentences:

Promotion should not be more important than ac-complishment; avoiding instability should not be more important than taking the risk.

The dash

Because it speeds the reader along, the dash has virtually replaced the colon (:). Written with one space on either side, the dash looks as if it might be an arrow pointing your reader's way to an important part of the sentence. In this sense, it is an effective way to attract and direct the reader's attention:

The business of government is to keep the government out of business—unless, of course, the business needs the government.

The dash can also serve the same function as parentheses. Parentheses offer high visibility, but they slow the reader down and look somewhat formal compared to dashes. Dashes give the impression of speech:

"The money getters—those to whom we owe our academies, colleges and churches—are the real benefactors of our race."

—P.T. Barnum.

The dash can be used to show attribution, as in the quotation by P.T. Barnum, and it can also be used to insert information before concluding the sentence:

The news of Edward R. Murrow's death— reportedly from cancer—was followed on CBS by a cigarette commercial.

The danger with dashes is that—because of their popularity—people tend to overuse them. There's nothing wrong with this—at least not yet—but too many dashes—as the sentences in this paragraph demonstrate—weaken the effect of the dash, slow the reader down and can rob other punctuation marks of their meaning and use.

The hyphen

Hyphens join two or more words, but the new word they form usually has a meaning different from what the words mean by themselves. The most common example is the word "basketball." When the two words were first joined, they were linked by a hyphen: "basketball." But repeated use of the new compound made the word so familiar that the hyphen could be dropped. The same is true for "skyscraper," "briefcase" and "airport."

Though dozens of words have made the transition from hyphenated compounds to single words, hundreds of others have not. These words have either not received the common usage of a word such as "basketball," or the absence of the hyphen could cause confusion. A dictionary is the best source for determining which compounds have made the passage to one word and which have not. Nevertheless, there are some guidelines to follow when hyphenating words.

Guidelines for Hyphens

Hyphenate two or more words functioning as a unit.

his never-say-never attitude (adjective)
his grip was a bone-crusher (noun)
the muggers pistol-whipped him (verb)

Note that, unlike the dash, hyphens are not separated from the words they connect by a space on either side.

Hyphenate two-word numbers when they are written out.

Twenty-one days from now, she will be here.

Hyphenate words that are combined with the prefixes "ex-" and "self-."

The ex-president felt very self-conscious.

Hyphenate prefixes like "anti-," "pro-" and "pre-" when the first letter of the next word begins with a capital letter.

She was anti-Establishment, but she was also pro-American.

Hyphenate words when not to do so would cause confusion.

re-cover (the chair) / recover (the lost wallet)
re-sign (the contract) / resign (from office)

Hyphenate words that are suspended in a sentence.

He will take a two- to four-year leave of absence.

If this kind of construction looks odd to you or you're not sure if what you've written is correct, consider rewriting the sentence:

He will take a leave of absence for two to four years.

The apostrophe

Use the apostrophe to form the plural case of a noun. Show possession with an " 's " for singular nouns and an "s' " for plural nouns.

singular nouns	plural nouns
manager's	managers'
president's	presidents'

Show possession with nouns that form their plural in ways other than by adding an "s" by adding " 's" to the plural of the noun.

singular nouns	plural nouns
man's	men's
woman's	women's
child's	children's

Show possession of singular nouns ending in "s" by adding an apostrophe or by adding an " 's."

singular nouns	plural nouns
boss's car	dress's button
boss' signature	dress' seam

Although less widely acceptable, you can also add an apostrophe.

> waitress' sandwich
> press' notebook

To show possession of plural nouns ending in "s," add an apostrophe to the end of the word.

> boys' frame
> executives' club
> writers' network

To form the possessive of pairs of nouns, add " 's" to the second noun in instances of joint possession:

> John and Mary's office
> the brother and sister's car
> the men and women's pool

Add " 's" to each member of the pair in instances of individual possession:

> John's and Mary's computers
> the brother's and sister's cars
> the men's and women's pools

To show possession for group nouns or compound nouns, add " 's" to the end of the unit:

group nouns	compound nouns
association's	editor-in-chief's
team's	someone else's
committee's	president-elect's

To show possession for compounds that form their plural by adding "s" to the first word, add 's to the end of the unit.

> editors-in-chief's
> sons-in-law's
> writers in residence's

Avoid confusion when adding an apostrophe to some plural words.

Jackson received two Es on his scorecard.
He now stirs drinks for the Oakland As.

What are the "do's" and "don'ts" here? Ask yourself what helps your reader best? Obviously "do's" is better than "dos"; "don'ts" is better than "donts"; "A's" is more effective than "As"; and "Es" is understandable left as is or written "E's."

The ellipsis

The ellipsis (three periods) indicates that a series of words has been omitted from a direct quotation:

The manager said, "Our customers ... are unhappy."

To show the deletion of whole sentences, add another period to the ellipsis:

The results are irrelevant .... A similar document could be produced to conclude the exact opposite.

The correct way to write an ellipsis is with one space on either side.

Quotation marks

Quotation marks can be used to emphasize a word or cite an example, but they have two main functions:

To show what someone said.

Albert Camus wrote, "The society of money and exploitation has never been charged, so far as I know, with assuring the triumph of freedom and justice."

On the other hand, Woodrow Wilson tells us, "Every great man of business has got somewhere a touch of the idealist in him."

To identify the title of a short story, poem, article, song, chapter in a book, one-act play or any other

short piece of writing. (Titles of longer works—books, plays, movies, newspapers and magazines—are commonly italicized or underlined.)

> "Raindrops Keep Falling on My Head" set just the right mood for William Goldman's *Butch Cassidy and the Sundance Kid.*

Quotation marks and other punctuation

The major problem with quotation marks comes when you mix them with periods, commas and question marks. This poses no problem for a sentence such as:

> *Yogi Berra said, "If people want to come out to the ballpark, nobody's going to stop them."*

But what if the speaker asks a question about the words in the quotation:

> *Did Yogi really say, "Nobody's going to stop them"?*

Periods and commas go inside the quotation marks; colons and semicolons go outside. Question marks may go inside or outside depending on who is doing the talking.

> *Did Yogi say, "Nobody is going to stop them"?*
> *She asked, "What did Yogi say?"*

Exclamations!

Don't use too many of them! Save them for when they count! Otherwise, like the boy who cried wolf, your exclamations won't be taken seriously!!!

11
Syntax

"All the fun's in how you say a thing."
—Robert Frost

Syntax is the way we arrange our words when we write or speak. If you're a native speaker of English, you know all you need to know about how to structure a sentence. You've been structuring sentences all your life. As long as you write as close as possible to the way you speak, you will almost always arrange your words in simple, clear, easy-to-understand sentences.

There are a few times, however, when help is needed. No one has difficulty with all of the syntax problems discussed in this chapter, but most people have trouble with one or two of them. After you've learned to correct the problems that appear most frequently in your writing, keep a special lookout for them when proofreading. These are the mistakes that business writers tend to make over and over again.

Subject-verb agreement

Singular subjects take singular verbs ("He goes to the office") and plural subject require plural verbs ("They go to the office"). But sometimes we place our verbs so far away from our subjects that we match our verbs with some other word in the sentence. This other word almost always is located between the subject and the verb. For example, we can express this thought with little difficulty:

The projections seem to be holding up.

"Seem" agrees in number with "projections." Problems occur, however, when we start placing words between "projections" and "seem." For example:

The projections, despite strong evidence, seems to be holding up.

Because "evidence," was the last word to come into my mind before writing the verb "seems." I incorrectly matched "seems" with "evidence" rather than with "projections," the word "seem" should refer to.

The most irritating thing about agreement problems is that we know better. Not only do we know that subjects and verbs have to match, we know how to match them. Unfortunately, we get distracted by the other words in the sentence.

Even when we're not distracted by other words in the sentence, there are certain situations that cause many people trouble:

Singular nouns joined by "and" require a plural verb because there are now two subjects in the sentence:

John and Mary arrive on time.

The few exceptions to this rule are almost all the expressions of a particular culture or dialect:

Rock 'n roll is here to stay.

Peanut butter and jelly is on the way.

In these cases, as in most others, your ear is the best judge for determining the most effective syntax.

Nouns joined by "or" or "nor" use singular verbs if all the nouns are singular:

Either John or Mary has to give in.

Nouns joined by "or" or "nor" use plural verbs if all the nouns are plural:

Neither the men nor the women want to submit.

When one noun is singular and the other noun is plural, the verb agrees in number with the closest noun.

Neither John nor the women want to continue.

Noun-pronoun agreement

Pronouns, which are substitutes for nouns, have two things in common with nouns: number (singular or plural) and gender (masculine, feminine or neuter). What they don't have in common is person. All nouns are third person, but some pronouns are first person ("I," "we"), some are second person ("you"), and some are third person ("he," "she," "it," "they," "one," "some," "none," "all," "everybody," "somebody").

A pronoun in any sentence must agree with the noun it refers to in person, number and gender.

Person: "The president assigned some sales people to the project, but she knew it wouldn't help." The neuter pronoun "it" cannot refer to "people." The correct pronoun is "they."

Number: "The testing of the new security devices should be nearing their final stage." The plural pronoun "their" cannot refer to the singular noun "testing." The correct pronoun is "its."

Gender: "The old car did her best, but the hill was too much." The feminine pronoun "her" should not be linked with a neuter noun. The correct pronoun is "its."

Mismatching nouns and pronouns in person and gender is not a common error; mismatching nouns and pronouns in number is. Much of the trouble involving number has to do with words such as "everyone," "everybody," "all," "none," "some" and "each."

"Everyone", "everybody", "anybody" and "anyone" take singular verbs and are referred to with singular pronouns:

"Anybody who enters must pay her fee by Friday."

All and some are singular or plural depending on the context they appear in. Both words are often followed by "of." If what comes after the "of" is a mass or bulk something, the pronoun is singular:

Some of the material has lost its color.

If what comes after the "of" refers to a number of things or persons, the pronoun is plural:

Some of the agents lost their notebooks.

Traditionally, "none" is singular or plural depending on the context, but the distinction of singular or plural within certain contexts is so subtle that either a singular or a plural pronoun would be correct:

None of the sales people was willing to submit his or her report.

Also correct is:

None of the sales people were willing to submit their reports.

On the other hand, the singular forms "was" and "his" would be hard to justify in this sentence:

None of the salespeople were as good as their managers.

"Each" is always singular:

Each renewed her personal dedication to increased sales.

Unless, of course, "each" refers to a group whose members are both male and female. In this case, the plural pronoun "they" is acceptable, but the more grammatically appropriate sentence would be:

The sales people renewed their dedication to increased sales.

Modifiers

A modifier is a word that changes or in some way alters the meaning of another word. For this reason, modifiers should be placed as close as possible to the words they modify. To put them somewhere else can cause readers to understand something different than intended.

Old and in disrepair, I bought the building cheap.

The building may be in better shape than the buyer.

The president of the company explained why coffee breaks were detrimental to business on Monday.

During the rest of the week coffee breaks were okay.

Read your sentences out loud. Your ear is a great aid in revealing the misplacement of modifying words and phrases.

Fragments

When we were in grammar school, we were taught that a sentence is a complete thought. It had a subject and a verb. We were also taught that a fragment was an incomplete thought. It lacked a subject or a verb and, therefore, it was unacceptable.

We pointed out to our teachers that many of the writers we were asked to read wrote in fragments. Were they wrong? We were told these writers had a poetic license, and when we were famous writers, we could write in fragments, too. Until that point, we would be required to write complete sentences.

The idea stuck with us and, as a result, many writers feel uncomfortable when they see a sentence fragment in print. What we have to realize is that fluent speakers of English write and converse in fragments all the time. They do this because each is capable of supplying the missing words.

The problem, then, is not fragments, but how they are used. When you use a fragment, make sure you have a specific purpose or effect in mind. Make sure your fragment communicates clearly what you want to say to your reader.

Although the report reached his desk on time ...

This is an ineffective fragment. There are too many missing words for the reader to supply.

The company was in a nose-dive. Until November. That's when Mike Flannagan took over.

"Until November" is an effective fragment; it emphasizes the date on which the company began its rebound.

I need your help. Now!

Like "Until November," "Now!" has neither a subject nor a predicate, but the powerful effect of the word could not have been achieved—or achieved as well—in a complete sentence.

The points to be made by these examples are:

1. Fragments are an ordinary, everyday part of the English language. In this sense, they are grammatically correct.
2. Fragments, when used properly, are not only an effective means of communication, they are stylistically desirable.

Run-on sentences

Sentences must be separated by a period, a semicolon or a conjunction. A run-on sentence joins two sentences without placing any punctuation or conjunction between them. This sentence joins two complete thoughts without a punctuation mark:

Wallace Stevens was a talented poet he was also the president of an insurance company.

This sentence joins two complete thoughts with a traditionally improper punctuation mark: the comma between poet and he. The name for this error is "comma splice."

Wallace Stevens was a talented poet, he was also the president of an insurance company.

To punctuate this sentence correctly in business writing, there are three possibilities:

1. Wallace Stevens was a talented poet. He was also the president of an insurance company.
2. Wallace Stevens was a talented poet; he was also the president of an insurance company.
3. Wallace Stevens was a talented poet, but he was also the president of an insurance company.

Parallel construction

Parallelism means using the same grammatical structure for all the items in a sentence that have the same function. Parallelism not only holds sentences together, it adds emphasis, provides flow, expresses thoughts more clearly, makes reading more pleasurable, takes up less space and makes what we say easy to remember. This is why so many famous quotations are in parallel forms:

I came, I saw, I conquered.

A penny saved is a penny earned.

Do unto others as you would have them do unto you.

Faulty parallelism occurs when the second or successive items in a parallel series do not fit the pattern established by the first item. For example:

Eating is time-consuming, costly and it makes you fat.

The proper construction for this sentence should be:

Eating is time-consuming, costly and fattening.

Correct faulty parallelism by putting all the related ideas into the same grammatical form.

Tense

Most verbs are written in the present, past or future tense. Sometimes, however, writing requires a shift from one tense to another. If, for example, we are contrasting past action with present action, or demanding action in the future based on what is taking place in the present, we need to shift tenses. Errors occur when we don't change the tense of the verb to fit the action we are expressing. Here's an example:

I asked the manager where I could get a copy of the report, and he tells me I will have to see the president.

This sentence unnecessarily shifts from the past to the present tense with the word "tells." The logical way to write this sentence is:

I asked the manager where I could get a copy of the report, and he told me I would have to see the president.

Generally speaking, if you begin writing in one tense, you should stay in that tense. If you have to change, consider beginning a new paragraph every time you shift tenses. A new paragraph alerts the reader that a change may be coming, and a new paragraph also helps your reader understand your message more clearly.

Transitions

A proper transition is necessary for coherence. There should be transitions between paragraphs, between sentences and even between words in long sentences. The best transitional device is a logical presentation of your ideas; there is simply no substitute for getting ideas into their proper order in the first place and avoiding interruptions or irrelevant details later.

Transitional words relate what we have said to what we are going to say. Readers rely heavily on transitional words to establish the logic of sentences and groups of sentences. Misuse of transitional words changes the meaning of the message. Consider the following sentence:

While she was only a child, Mary could solve problems in algebra.

Does this mean that Mary is a child or that she was a child. If Mary is no longer a child, a more effective transition would be "when"; if Mary is a child, "although" would be a less confusing choice then "while."

When she was only a child, Mary could solve problems in algebra.

Although she was only a child, Mary could solve problems in algebra.

The careless use of "and" or "but" also detracts from clarity:

I bought a typewriter, and Dean bought a computer.

I bought a typewriter, but Dean bought a computer.

"And" means "in addition to"; "but" implies some kind of contrast or something contrary to what was expected. Choose the transition that conveys the exact meaning you intend.

If the reader doesn't understand what you are saying, no amount of tinkering to achieve emphasis or variety can salvage the writing. Have something to say and say it in an organized way. If a piece of writing has no focus, even an effective transition will not give it one.

Capitalization

Capitalization is determined by convention. Unless you have a specific reason for not doing so, obey the conventions. Here are some guidelines that can help:

- Capitalize the first word of every sentence.
- Capitalize the proper names of people, places and things: Bob, New York, the White House.
- Capitalize words derived from proper names: American, Edwardian.
- Capitalize the days of the week: Monday.
- Capitalize the months of the year: March, May.
- Capitalize names of holidays: Thanksgiving.

- Capitalize historical documents: Declaration of Independence.

- Capitalize historical events and ages: Reformation.

- Capitalize common names with place names: Mississippi River, Fifth Avenue.

- Capitalize the main words in titles: Moby Dick, The New York Times.

- Capitalize titles of offices when used directly before a name: Senator Kennedy, President Bush.

- Capitalize the words "president" and "governor" if they refer to the President of the United States or the Governor of a state.

- Capitalize "vice" when used in front of a name: Vice President Quayle.

- Capitalize the names of family members when used with a name: Uncle Bob, Grandma Moses.

Abbreviations

Abbreviations are seldom used in formal writing. Nevertheless, here are some guidelines:

1. Omit the period after each letter of an organization: CCNY (City College of New York), ROTC (Reserve Officers Training Corps), HEW (Health, Education, and Welfare).

2. Not all abbreviations are written the same way: MPH (miles per hour) can be written mph, Mph, m.p.h. If your company doesn't have a specific preference, choose the way you like best. Make sure, however, that you are consistent throughout any memo or letter you write.

Some common abbreviations

a.m.	ante meridiem, before noon
p.m.	post meridiem, after noon
e.g.	exempli gratia, for example
i.e.	id est, that is
ibid.	ibidem, in the same place
etc.	et cetera, and so forth

Acronyms

An acronym is a special kind of abbreviation. It is formed by the first letter or letters of each word in a name or phrase. CIA, for example, is an acronym for Central Intelligence Agency, and sonar is an acronym for sound navigation ranging. Some acronyms are pronounced as if they were independent words. The acronym for North Atlantic Treaty Organization, for example, is pronounced as the word "NATO"; we don't pronounce each individual letter and say "N-A-T-O."

The use of acronyms has increased greatly in the twentieth century, but not everyone knows every acronym. Unless the acronym is used in everyday speech ("DNA" instead of "deoxyribonucleic acid"), spell out the complete word or title on first reference and place the acronym immediately afterwards in a set of parentheses. Then you may use the acronym for all future references.

Jose Rodriguez began working for Minnesota Mining and Manufacturing (3M) in 1964. Today he is vice-president of 3M Research and Development.

Numerals

Numbers in writing are governed by convention. The standard guidelines are listed below, however, your company's or subject field's policies may vary. Spell out numbers one through nine:

There were four people in the meeting.

Use the number for numerals 10 and above unless the word for that number is shorter or easier to read than the number itself:

There were 14 people at the meeting.
He sold the company for a million dollars.

Do not begin a sentence with an Arabic numeral:

600 employees work for Acme, Inc.

This sentence should be written:

Six hundred employees work for Acme, Inc.
A total of 600 employees work for Acme, Inc.

Spell out numbers under 101 when used as adjectives.

In the early twentieth century, there were fewer four-year colleges.

Don't spell out dates or numbers belonging to a series:

September 19, 1961.
Chapter II

Use Arabic numbers with a.m. and p.m. Use "o'clock" and "morning" or "afternoon" when the number is in script.

The meeting went to 7 p.m.
The meeting went to seven in the evening.
The meeting went to seven o'clock in the evening.

12

Grammar Hotlines

The following grammar hotlines provide free answers to short questions about writing, grammar, punctuation, spelling, diction and syntax. Most of these services are staffed by faculty members, graduate students, editors and former teachers.

Changes may occur during the year, and hours of operation vary according to teaching schedules. Most of the hotlines either reduce or suspend service during college breaks and summer terms. Unless noted otherwise, services will not accept collect calls and will return long-distance calls collect only.

ALABAMA

Auburn
205-844-4000—Writing Center Hotline
Monday-Thursday, 9 a.m. to noon and 1 p.m. to 4
p.m.; Friday, 9 a.m. to noon; same during summer
Auburn University

Jacksonville
205-782-5409—Grammar Hotline
Monday-Friday, 8 a.m. to 4:30 p.m.
Jacksonville State University

Tuscaloosa
205-348-5049—Grammar Hotline
Monday-Thursday, 8:30 a.m. to 4 p.m.;
Sunday, Tuesday and Wednesday, 6 p.m. to 9
p.m.; Friday, 8:30 a.m. to 2 p.m.
University of Alabama

ARKANSAS

Little Rock
501-569-3162—The Writer's Hotline
Monday-Friday, 8 a.m. to 11 a.m.
University of Arkansas at Little Rock

CALIFORNIA

Moorpark
805-378-1494—National Grammar Hotline
Monday-Friday, 8 a.m. to noon, August to June; 24-
hour answering machine
Moorpark College

Sacramento
916-688-7444—English Help Line
Time varies each semester; 24-hour answering
machine
Cosumnes River College

COLORADO

Pueblo
719-549-2787—USC Grammar Hotline
Monday-Friday, 9:30 a.m. to 3:30 p.m., September to
May; 24-hour answering machine
University of Southern Colorado

DELAWARE

Newark
302-831-1890—Grammar Hotline
Monday-Thursday, 9 a.m. to 5 p.m. and 6 p.m. to 9
p.m.; Friday, 9 a.m. to 5 p.m.
University of Delaware

FLORIDA

Coral Gables
305-284-2956—Grammar Hotline
Monday-Friday, 8:30 a.m. to 5 p.m.; occasional
evening hours
University of Miami

Ft. Lauderdale
305-475-6596—Grammar Hotline
Monday-Friday, 8 a.m. to 4 p.m.
Broward Community College—Central Campus

Pensacola
904-474-2129—Writing Lab and Grammar Hotline
Monday-Friday, 9 a.m. to 4 p.m.; Tuesday to 9 p.m.
University of West Florida

GEORGIA

Atlanta
404-651-2000—Writing Center
Monday-Thursday, opens 8 a.m.; Friday, opens 10 a.m.
Georgia State University

Rome
706-295-6312—Grammar Hotline
Monday-Friday, 8:30 a.m. to 5 p.m.
Floyd College

ILLINOIS

Charleston
217-581-5929—Grammar Hotline
Monday-Friday, 10 a.m. to 3 p.m.; summer hours,
June 14-August 4, Monday-Thursday, 8 a.m. to 3
p.m.
Eastern Illinois University

Des Plaines

708-635-1948—The Write Line: "Dr. Grammar"
Monday-Friday, 9:30 a.m. to 2 p.m.
Oakton Community College

Normal

309-438-2345—Grammar Hotline
Monday-Thursday, 9 a.m. to 4 p.m.; Friday, 9 a.m. to
3 p.m.
Illinois State University

Oglesby

815-224-2720—Grammarline
Monday-Friday, 8 a.m. to 4 p.m.
Illinois Valley Community College

Palatine

708-397-3000, ext. 2389—Grammar "Right" Line
Monday-Friday, 10 a.m. to 1 p.m.; 24-hour answering
machine; calls returned
William Rainey Harper College

River Grove

708-456-0300, ext. 254—Grammarphone
Monday-Thursday, 8 a.m. to 2 p.m. and 4 p.m. to 8
p.m.; Friday, 8 a.m. to 2 p.m.
Triton College

INDIANA

Indianapolis

317-274-3000—IUPUI Writing Center Hotline
Monday-Friday, 9 a.m. to 4 p.m.; summer hours,
Monday, Wednesday and Friday, 8:30 a.m. to
3 p.m.
Indiana University—Purdue University at Indianapolis

Muncie
317-285-8387—Grammar Crisis Line
Monday-Thursday 10 a.m. to 7 p.m.; Friday, 10 a.m.
to 5 p.m., September to May; summer hours,
Monday-Thursday 10 a.m. to 2 p.m.; Friday, 11
a.m. to 1 p.m.
Ball State University

West Lafayette
317-494-3723—Grammar Hotline
Monday-Friday, 9 a.m. to 4 p.m.; until June 9,
Tuesday-Thursday, noon to 2 p.m.; June 13-August
4, Monday-Thursday, 11 a.m. to 1 p.m. and 2 p.m. to
4 p.m.
Purdue University

KANSAS

Emporia
316-343-1200—Writer's Hotline
Monday-Friday, 11 a.m. to 4 p.m. and 7 p.m. to 9 p.m.
Emporia State University

Overland Park
913-469-8500, ext. 3439—Grammar Hotline
Monday-Thursday, 8 a.m. to 8 p.m.
Johnson County Community College

LOUISIANA

Lafayette
318-231-5224—Grammar Hotline
Monday-Thursday, 8 a.m. to 4 p.m.; Friday, 8 a.m. to
3 p.m.; summer hours, Monday-Friday, 8 a.m. to
3 p.m.
University of Southwestern Louisiana

MARYLAND

Baltimore
410-455-3052—Writer's Hotline
Monday-Friday, 11 a.m. to 1 p.m., September to May
University of Maryland—Baltimore County

Emmitsburg
301-447-5367—Grammar Hotline
Monday-Friday, 9 a.m. to 4 p.m.
Mount St. Mary's College

Frostburg
301-689-4327—Grammar Hotline
Monday-Friday, 10 a.m. to noon; no summer hours
Frostburg State College

MASSACHUSETTS

Boston
617-373-2512—Grammar Hotline
Monday-Thursday, 8:30 a.m. to 4 p.m.
Northeastern University

Lynn
617-593-7284—Grammar Hotline
Monday-Friday, 8:30 a.m. to 4 p.m.
North Shore Community College

MICHIGAN

Flint
313-762-0229—Grammar Hotline
Monday-Thursday, 10 a.m. to 1 p.m. and 4 p.m. to
    5:45 p.m.; no summer hours
C.S. Mott Community College

Kalamazoo
616-387-4442—Writer's Hotline
Monday-Friday, 1 p.m. to 4 p.m.
Western Michigan University

Lansing
517-483-1040—Writer's Hotline
Monday-Friday, 9 a.m. to 4 p.m.
Lansing Community College

MISSOURI

Joplin
417-624-0171—Grammar Hotline
Monday-Friday, 9 a.m. to 2 p.m.; summer
    session hours, Monday-Thursday, 7:30 a.m.
    to 1 p.m.
Missouri Southern State College

Kansas City
816-235-2244—Writer's Hotline
Monday-Friday, 9 a.m. to 4 p.m.
University of Missouri at Kansas City

Springfield
417-836-6398—Writer's Hotline
Monday, 9 a.m. to 4 p.m.; Tuesday, Wednesday and
    Thursday, 9 a.m. to 5 p.m.; Friday, 9 a.m. to
    1 p.m.
Southwest Missouri State University

St. Louis
314-367-8700, ext. 244—St. LCOP Writer's Hotline
Monday-Friday, 9 a.m. to 5 p.m.
St. Louis College of Pharmacy

NEW JERSEY

Jersey City
201-200-3337/-3338—Grammar Hotline
Monday-Friday, 9 a.m. to 4:30 p.m.; summer hours,
   Monday-Thursday, 8 a.m. to 5 p.m.
Jersey City State College

NORTH CAROLINA

Fayetteville
919-630-7000—Grammar Hotline
Monday-Friday, 9 a.m. to 4 p.m.
Methodist College

Greenville
919-757-6399—Grammar Hotline
Monday-Thursday, 9 a.m. to 8 p.m.; Friday, 9 a.m. to
   2 p.m.; evening hours vary
East Carolina University

OHIO

Ashland
419-289-5110—Ashland University Writing Center
Monday-Friday, 8 a.m. to 5 p.m.
Ashland University

Cincinnati
513-745-5731—Dial-A-Grammar
Monday-Friday, 9 a.m. to 4 p.m.;
   24-hour answering machine; calls returned
Raymond Walters College

513-569-1500, ext. 1736—Writing Center Hotline
Monday-Thursday, 8 a.m. to 8 p.m.; Friday, 8 a.m. to
   4 p.m.; Saturday, 9 a.m. to 1 p.m.
Cincinnati Technical College

Cleveland
216-987-2050—Grammar Hotline
Monday-Friday, 10 a.m. to noon; Monday-Thursday,
   6 p.m. to 8 p.m.; 24-hour answering machine
Cuyahoga Community College

Dayton
513-873-2158—Writer's Hotline
Monday-Friday, 9 a.m. to 4 p.m., September 1 to June 1
Wright State University

Delaware
614-368-3925—Writing Resource Center
Monday-Friday, 9 a.m. to noon and 1 p.m. to 4 p.m.,
   September to May; no summer hours
Ohio Wesleyan University

Orrville
216-683-2010—Grammar Hotline
Monday-Thursday, 9 a.m. to 5 p.m.; Friday, 9 a.m. to
   noon; Saturday, 10 a.m. to noon
University of Akron—Wayne College

OKLAHOMA

Bethany
405-491-6328—Grammar Hotline
Monday-Friday, 9 a.m. to 4 p.m.; June, July and
   August call 405-722-8883
Southern Nazarene University

Chickasha

405-224-8622—Grammar Hotline
Monday-Friday, 9 a.m. to 5 p.m.; Saturday, 9 a.m. to noon
Virginia Lee Underwood (Mrs. Underwood, retired teacher and editor, offers this service through her home telephone. She is willing to return long-distance calls collect.)

OREGON

Portland

503-725-3570—Writing Helpline
Monday-Friday, 10 a.m. to 3 p.m.; voice mail
Portland State University Writing Lab

PENNSYLVANIA

Allentown

215-437-4471—Academic Support Center
Monday-Friday, 10 a.m. to 3 p.m., September to May 15
Cedar Crest College

Glen Mills

215-399-1130—Burger Associates
Monday-Friday, 8 a.m. to 5 p.m.
Robert S. Burger (Mr. Burger, formerly a teacher of writing and journalism at several colleges, offers this service through his office, which conducts courses in effective writing.)

Philadelphia

215-204-5612—Writer's Helpline
Monday-Friday, 8:30 a.m. to 4:30 p.m.; 24-hour answering machine
Temple University

Pittsburgh
412-344-9759—Grammar Hotline
Monday-Friday, 9 a.m. to 5 p.m.; 24-hour answering
machine
Chatham College

SOUTH CAROLINA

Charleston
803-953-3194—Grammar Hotline
Monday-Friday, 8 a.m. to 5 p.m.; Sunday-Thursday,
7 p.m. to 10 p.m.; summer hours, Monday-Friday,
9 a.m. to 5 p.m.
The Citadel Writing Center

Spartansburg
803-596-9613 or 596-9186—Writer's Hotline
Monday-Thursday, 1:15 p.m. to 6 p.m.; morning and
evening hours vary
Converse College

TEXAS

Amarillo
806-374-4726—Grammarphone
Monday-Thursday, 8 a.m. to 9 p.m.; Friday, 8 a.m. to 3 p.m.
Amarillo College

Houston
713-221-8670—University of Houston Downtown
Grammar Line
Monday-Thursday, 9 a.m. to 4 p.m.; Friday, 9 a.m. to
1 p.m.; summer hours, Monday-Thursday, 10:30
a.m. to 4 p.m.
University of Houston Downtown

San Antonio
210-733-2503—Learning Line
Monday-Friday, 8 a.m. to 8 p.m.; summer hours vary
San Antonio College

VIRGINIA

Sterling
703-450-2511—Interdisciplinary Writing Center
Monday-Friday, 9 a.m. to 3 p.m.; various additional
daytime and evening hours
Northern Virginia Community College Loudoun Campus

Virginia Beach
804-427-7170—Grammar Hotline
Monday-Friday, 10 a.m. to noon; afternoon hours vary;
summer hours, Monday, 1 p.m.-2 p.m.; Tuesday, 10
a.m.-12:30 p.m.; Wednesday, 3 p.m.-5 p.m.;
Thursday, 10:30 a.m.-1 p.m.; Friday, 9 a.m.-10 a.m.
Tidewater Community College Writing Center

WEST VIRGINIA

Montgomery
304-442-3119—Writer's Hotline
Monday-Friday, 8 a.m. to 4:30 p.m.; 24-hour
answering machine
West Virginia Institute of Technology

WISCONSIN

Platteville
608-342-1615—Grammar Hotline (if no answer, 342-1826)
Monday-Friday, 8 a.m. to 4 p.m.; 24-hour answering
machine
University of Wisconsin—Platteville

Stevens Point
715-346-3528—Writer's Hotline
Monday-Thursday, 9 a.m. to 4 p.m.; Friday, 9 a.m. to
    noon
University of Wisconsin—Stevens Point
    Tutoring-Learning Center

CANADA

Edmonton, Alberta
403-497-5663—Grammar Hotline
Monday-Friday, 9 a.m. to 11 a.m. and 1 p.m. to 3 p.m.
Grant McEwan Community College

13

Writing for Business

"Every style that is not boring is a good one."
—Voltaire

Make business writing conversational

Most of what we find dull in business correspondence isn't what we say but how we say it. Just because we work for an institution is no reason why we have to sound like one. The most effective business correspondence, like the best writing anywhere, is short, clear and personal. Phrases such as "prioritized evaluative procedures" and "modified departmental agenda" only make readers work harder to understand the message.

Before writing any memo or letter, ask yourself this important question: Is this necessary? One of the secrets to writing effective memos and letters is limiting yourself to correspondence that counts. Most memos and letters are too long, sent to too many people and written by people who write too many of them. They also take time and energy to write. Telephoning, in many cases, is faster, more personal and more effective. If there are any questions, you can answer them right away. Correspondence, on the other hand, can't adjust to a reader's reaction the way a speaker adjusts to a listener's. Nor can you change what you've written once you've sent it out.

An advantage of memos and letters is that they force us to articulate our thoughts. People can read them again if they're unsure about something. They can show them to others to help eliminate hearsay and rumors.

Memos and letters also have a way of encouraging others to act. People may deliberately avoid running into us or forget what we said to them on the phone, but they have a harder time ignoring something that's staring up at them from the desk and waiting for them. They know the only way to get rid of that memo or letter is to act on it.

For this reason, written correspondence saves time. It's not as easy as talking on the phone, but it enables us to reach more people simultaneously and, if it is well written, we won't have to repeat ourselves.

Finally, written correspondence makes for good public relations. It gets our name seen, makes sure we get credit for our ideas, proves our ability to express ourselves and frees us to complete other tasks.

Memos and letters

No one has to work long in the business world to discover that writing is the universal currency for documenting what gets done and for formally expressing ideas. Every business person is by definition also a writer.

Write the most effective memos/letters

1. Determine what you want to say and to whom you are saying it.

What

Don't be afraid to discuss your ideas with colleagues. Discussion not only helps you clarify what you want to say and how you want to say it; it also helps generate new ideas.

Whom

What are my audience's needs?

How much of what I want to say is relevant?

Does what I have to say make a significant contribution to the reader's work?

What's the best tone or approach to use for this particular reader or audience?

What specific examples would best help my reader understand my message faster and respond more effectively?

2. Construct an outline of what you want to say.

Collect and review any relevant literature or previous documentation you can find that is related to your subject.

Arrange all your ideas in a clear, logical order.

Get feedback from a colleague on the information you've selected as most important and how effectively you've ordered this information in your outline.

3. Write.

Sections of any memo or letter do not necessarily have to be written in sequence. Consider starting with the easiest sections; then, once you've warmed up, go into more difficult parts. Don't be a prisoner of your outline. Explore your thoughts. See where they might lead. Experiment with how different words and phrases sound.

Don't be afraid to cut a section and start it over again. Sometimes, our words just won't bend to the thoughts we have in mind. Back off and try a new approach.

4. Revise.

Again, don't be afraid to consult with a colleague. Ask yourself and your colleague these specific questions:

Is it short, clear and personal? In a study of 800 letters, written by the top chief executive officers in the United States, all letters were short, clear and personal. All the participants claimed they didn't get to be CEOs by writing letters the way other people told them business letters should sound. Each found out through his or her own experiences that the most effective letters were short, clear and personal and, by the time they became CEOs, they never once sent out a letter that didn't contain these three basic principles of good writing.

How effective is your writing

Are my ideas arranged effectively? In some cases, a chronological order is called for, in others, a step-by-step process. If you have a choice in determining your letter's order, consider this: people remember best what they read first; they remember second best what they read last.

Does my opening sentence grab the reader's attention? Consider writing it last. Once you have what you want to say on paper, go back and write an opening sentence that is short, clear, simple, easy to understand, grabs the reader's attention and makes the reader want to keep reading.

Writing the opening sentence last is much faster, easier and more effective than trying to come up with a sentence that covers what you're trying to say before you've even said it.

Is my concluding sentence effective? Second in importance only to a good opening sentence, the concluding sentence is a good opportunity to induce some action on the part of the reader. Consider these concluding sentences:

> *As soon as we hear from you, we will ...*
> *Will you please let us know if ...*
> *Can you arrange to ...*
> *I'll call you next Thursday to see ...*

Would any headings, lists, tables or graphs help clarify my meaning? Concrete language and personal details are two ways of being specific, but nothing helps the images these words create in our minds as much as a good heading, list, table or graph.

The headings of this book offer good examples of how headings work. Open to any page. Notice how, before you begin to read a word on that page, your eyes are drawn to the heading?

Lists serve the same function as headings. They draw the reader's eyes onto the page and can suggest that there are a finite number of points to consider.

For the best examples of tables and graphs, consider any issue of *USA Today*. Each issue includes first-rate examples of how tables and graphs can be attractively and effectively presented.

Is it correct? Not just the information but the spelling of the reader's name. You'd be surprised at the difference a correctly spelled name makes in a reader's attitude toward you and your subject.

Is my name legible? Your signature is the most personal part of any letter. Sign it with a pen you enjoy using and make it legible.

Is the postscript handwritten? Handwritten postscripts are often read before and then again after the letter is read. Be careful, however, that what you put in a postscript isn't so important as to make you look forgetful or careless.

Have I correctly addressed my reader? Here are some common titles, addresses and proper salutations:

Title	Address on Envelope	Salutation in Letter
1. Admiral	Adm. (name), USN	Dear Admiral (name)
2. Ambassador	The Honorable (name)	Dear Mr./Ms. Ambassador
3. Archbishop	Most Rev. (name)	Dear Archbishop (name)
4. Archdeacon	The Venerable (name)	Venerable Sir or Madam
5. Attorney General	Hon. (name)	Dear Mr./Ms. (name)
6. Attorney	Mr./Ms. (name)	Dear Mr./Ms. (name)
7. Bishop (Catholic)	Most Rev. (name)	Dear Bishop (name)
8. Bishop (other)	Right Rev. (name)	Dear Bishop (name)
9. Colonel	Col.(name), USA, USAF, USMC	Dear Col. (name)
10. Commodore	Com. (name), USCG, USN	Dear Commodore (name)
11. Congressman	The Honorable (name)	Dear Mr./Ms. (name)
12. Consul	The (country) Consul	Dear Mr./Ms. (name)
13. Dean (church)	The Very Rev.	Very Rev. Sir or Madam
14. Dean (college)	Dean (name)	Dear Dean (name)
15. General	Gen. (name)	Dear Gen. (name)
16. Governor	The Honorable (name)	Dear Governor (name)
17. Judge	The Honorable (name)	Dear Judge (name)
18. Mayor	The Honorable (name)	Dear Mayor (name)
19. Minister (consul)	Hon. (name)	Dear Mr./Ms. (name)
20. Minister (clergy)	The Rev (name)	Dear Mr./Ms. (name)
21. Monsignor	The Right Rev. (name)	Dear Monsignor (name)
22. The Pope	His Holiness, Pope (name)	Your Holiness
23. Postmaster General	Hon. (name)	Dear Mr./Ms.
24. President (college)	Pres. (name, Ph.D.)	Dear Dr.
25. President (USA)	The President	Dear Mr./Ms. President
26. Priest	The Rev. (name)	Dear Father (name)
27. Principal	Dr./Mr./Mrs. (name)	Dear Dr./Mr./Mrs. (name)
28. Professor	Prof./ Dr. (name)	Dear Prof./Dr.
29. Rabbi	Rabbi (name)	Dear Rabbi (name)
30. Rector	The Very Rev. (name)	Dear Father (name)
31. Senator (USA)	The Hon. (name)	Dear Senator (name)
32. Sister	Sister (name)	Dear Sister (name)
33. Vice-President (USA)	The Hon. (name)	Dear Mr./Ms. Vice-President

Reports and proposals

There are many kinds of reports and proposals, but most have one thing in common: to help someone make a decision. Ask the right questions. The more narrow your focus, the less abstract your job will be.

What's the purpose of this report or proposal?

Who's going to read it?

What needs to be determined?

When did the problem start?

Have any attempts been made to correct it?

What are the causes of the problem?

What keeps the problem from being solved?

After you've finished writing your report or proposal, ask yourself these four questions:

1. Have I provided the reader with all the necessary documentation?
2. Are my findings presented clearly at the beginning and end of the report or proposal?
3. Have I answered any questions that may come to the reader's mind?
4. Have I anticipated any objections?

Once you've written your report or proposal, plug what you've written into this or a similar format:

The title page. The title page should include the company's name, your name and the date on which the report or proposal is submitted. The title of the report or proposal should be written in capital letters. Follow company policy or your own judgment for titles of individual chapters, charts and graphs.

Titles and subheads written in all capital letters are usually difficult to read, so use sparingly sentences in which every word is capitalized. An effective way to set subheads apart from the main body of any report or proposal is to capitalize only the first letter of each major word. Articles and prepositions such as the following, however, should be written in lower case:

a	an	as
at	but	by
for	if	in
on	or	
the	to	

The table of contents. Though not always necessary, it can be helpful to the readers of your lengthy reports and proposals that contain many subsections.

The summary or abstract. This is a one-page condensation that states explicitly your conclusions and recommendations.

The introduction. Include a statement about the purpose of your report or proposal and your view of the problem or situation. Also include your conclusions and recommendations, but don't write them in the same way they appear in the abstract. Consider including the limitations of your report or proposal, the methods used to gather the information and any definitions of unfamiliar terms.

The discussion. The main body of your report or proposal should state your case, substantiate your points with specific details and allow your reader to see the thought processes that led you to your conclusions and recommendations.

The conclusion. Discuss the relevance of your findings and any patterns or trends you discovered in your study that will help the reader with his or her decision about the subject.

The recommendation. Tell the reader how to put your conclusion into action.

The bibliography. The bibliography lists the books and articles referred to in the report or proposal. Bibliography entries are usually arranged in alphabetical order by the author's last name:

> Booth, Wayne C. *The Rhetoric of Fiction*. Chicago, IL: University of Chicago Press, 1961.
>
> Frye, Northrop. *Anatomy of Criticism: Four Essays*. Princeton, NJ: Princeton University Press, 1957.

If the author isn't known, use the first word of the title or article. If the title begins with "A" or "The," use the second word. Two or more books by the same author should appear in the bibliography as:

> Frye, Northrop. *Anatomy of Criticism: Four Essays*. Princeton, NJ: Princeton University Press, 1957.
> *The Critical Path: An Essay on the Social Context of Literary Criticism*. Bloomington, IN: Indiana University Press, 1971.

Articles and stories are written as:

> Levin, Yu. D. "Tolstoy, Shakespeare, and Russian Writers of the 1860's." *Oxford Slavonic Papers*, January 1985, pp. 15-23.

If the article or story appears within a chapter of a book, write:

> Wright, Richard. "Bright and Morning Star." In *Short Stories: A Critical Anthology*. Ed. Ensaf Thune and Ruth Prigozy. New York, NY: Macmillan, 1973.

Cassette tapes are written the same way as books:

Anderson, Richard. *Powerful Business Writing Skills*. Shawnee Mission, KS: National Press Publications, Inc., 1987.

Sections within a cassette tape are written the same way as articles:

Anderson, Richard. "How to Write a Complaint Letter," *Powerful Business Writing Skills*. Shawnee Mission, KS: National Press Publications, Inc., 1987.

The appendix. This section presents any data needed to support or expand upon the points made in the main body of your report or proposal.

The index. Necessary only in lengthy or complicated cases, the index is a detailed table of contents. It lists in alphabetical order almost every subject discussed in your report or proposal.

"Foolish consistency is the hobgoblin of little minds."

—Ralph Waldo Emerson

Equations. Don't try to record them on a typewriter or computer that isn't equipped with the necessary characters. Instead, leave space for any equations you will need and write them out long-hand later. If your document is to be printed, your equations will be typeset or penned in neatly by hand.

To make your equations stand out, consider positioning them on a separate line in the text. Introduce equations as you would any words that form a part of a sentence:

The current in the wire is calculated by using Ohm's law:

$E=IR$

Academic degrees. Professors holding the Ph.D. degree are commonly addressed as "Professor" or "Dr." Occasionally, the title is left out and "Ph.D." follows the name instead. The important thing to remember is to choose one form or the other; do not combine them. "Prof. Bernard Bell, Ph.D." is a redundant title. If the holder of the Ph.D. is not affiliated with the college or university you are referring to, address him or her as "Dr."

Complimentary close. Complimentary closes should be followed by commas and only the first word needs to be capitalized:

Sincerely,   Cordially,

Sincerely yours,   With best regards,

Yours truly,

Corrections and insertions. Avoid these as much as possible; make your memo, letter, report or proposal look as good as it can. If you have to make a correction or insert a word or phrase, do it in type or ink directly above the line involved. Don't use the margins or write below the line.

Ragged or justified margins. Justified looks better, but ragged is easier to read.

Dates. Don't abbreviate dates in a formal letter, report or proposal. Sept. 19th and 9/19/89 are not acceptable; 19 September 1989 and September 19, 1989 are.

Endnotes and footnotes. Endnotes appear at the end of a report or proposal; footnotes appear at the bottom of a page in a report or proposal. Both refer to something on the page which cites them. Both list their works the same way a bibliography does except for five things:

1. The first line is indented.

2. The author's first name precedes his or her last.

3. There is not a period after the title of the work.

4. The section containing information about the publisher is placed in parentheses.

5. The pages from which the quotation is taken or the reference is made are listed.

Footnote:

Robert Scholes. *The Nature of Narrative* (New York: Oxford University Press, 1966), pp. 305.

Bibliography:

Scholes, Robert. *The Nature of Narrative.* New York, NY: Oxford University Press, 1966.

Margins. Keep the same width for the right-hand and left-hand margins.

Pagination. Number pages consecutively in the upper right-hand corner or centered at the bottom of the page. Do not punctuate them by adding periods. Although the title page and the first page of the text are not numbered, the pages are still counted. The bibliography and index pages are numbered.

Permissions. Although copyright holders may legally charge a fee for the reproduction of copyrighted material, U.S. copyright law states that "fair use" of a copyrighted work for the purposes of "criticism, comment, new reporting, teaching, scholarship or research" is not an infringement of copyright. If you're not planning to publish your report or proposal or make money from it, you don't need permission from an author to quote from his or her work.

Salutations. "Dear Mr. Jones" and "Dear Ms. Smith" are most commonly recommended; "Dear Sir:"

and "Gentlemen:" are not. If you don't know the name of the person you're writing to, write "Dear Sir or Madam:" If you know the name but don't know if the reader is male or female, leave out the salutation, replace it with a subject heading or write "Dear (person's name)." Use "Mrs." only if your reader indicates that she prefers "Mrs." to "Ms." She can indicate this preference by typing "Mrs." along with her full name under her signature.

Spacing. Anything longer than a letter should be double-spaced, including quotations and notes.

Syllabication. When a word must be divided at the end of a line, consult a dictionary if you are not absolutely sure where to divide the word.

Typing and paper. Clean type is essential. Avoid script or fancy print. Type on only one side of 8 1/2" x 11" good quality paper. Do not submit anything on "erasable" paper as it smudges easily and looks cheap.

A final word about form

Unlike the rules of spelling, policies regarding form change from year to year. If you're not sure what to do and there's no office grammarian around to ask, rely on common sense. Then, once you've made your decision, stick to it. Your consistency will often lead others not to question—they'll assume you must be right—or they'll wonder if they are wrong. So many people have consistently written "alright" instead of "all right" that the new edition of Webster's Dictionary lists both spellings as acceptable. However, the preferred spelling is always listed first.

A Final Checklist

"If any person wishes to write in a clear style, let him first be clear in his thoughts."

—Goethe

Before sending out anything—memo, letter, report or proposal—ask yourself these questions:

1. What's the purpose?

2. Have I said what I'm trying to say?

3. Does the message look good on the page?

4. Is it mechanically correct or at least consistent?

5. Have I checked any spellings, divided words, capitalizations, abbreviations and punctuations I'm not sure of?

6. Have I varied the length of the paragraphs and sentences to help keep the reader awake?

7. Are my ideas simply stated and presented in a clear, logical order?

8. Have I limited myself to one idea to each paragraph?

9. Is the letter as short as I can get it?

10. Are there unnecessary words I can eliminate?

11. Have I chosen the best words to say what I want to say?

12. Is what I've written "reader-centered" as opposed to "author-centered?"

13. Have I tried to turn my negatives into positives?

14. Have I maintained my respect for the reader?

15. Have I eliminated all clichés, jargon, buzz words and bureaucratic phrases?

16. Have I written in my natural voice?

17. Does the closing leave the reader with the main idea and inspire him or her to act?

Glossary

Acronym A word formed from the first letters in a title or the first letters in a group of words: "AIDS" is an acronym for "Acquired Immune Deficiency Syndrome."

Active verb An active verb tells us that the subject of the sentence is doing the action. "John hit the ball." John is the subject; John is doing the action.

Adjective A word that modifies or helps describe a noun. "John used a large bat."

Adverb A word that modifies a verb, an adjective or another adverb.

"John ran fast." The word "fast" modifies

Apostrophe A sign (') used to indicate letters that are left out of a word (can't), to show possession (the dog's bone), or to show the plurals of abbreviation. (Several Ph.D.'s met in the corner.)

Comma A sign (,) used to indicate division in a sentence (Mary is a chemist, and John is a librarian), to separate items in a list (John returned with apples, oranges and grapes), to mark off thousands in numerals (1,582) and to separate types of information in bibliographical data (Brattleboro, Vermont: Amana Books, 1989).

Conjunction A word used to connect words or groups of words.

"John and Mary." The conjunction "and" connects the words "John" and "Mary."

"Benjamin Franklin tells us to write things worth doing or do things worth writing." The conjunction "or" connects the group of words "write things worth doing" and "do things worth writing."

Cliché A word or expression that has lost its power through overuse. "Strong as an ox" is one example. Others include:

"Pursuant to..."
"In reference to your letter of..."
"As per your request..."
"Enclosed herewith please find..."

Contraction The shortened form of a word ("can't" for "can not") or a group of words ("I'm" for "I am").

Euphemism The substitution of a mild, vague or general word for one considered too direct, harsh or blunt. "To pass away" is a euphemism for "to die."

Fragments Words and phrases that cannot stand alone because they do not express complete thoughts. "As we lay awake listening to the river" is not a complete thought. Something has to follow to make this thought complete: "As we lay awake listening to the river, a bear appeared."

Gender The three groups into which all English nouns fall: masculine, feminine and neuter.

Infinitive An infinitive phrase is a verb with the word "to" in front of it: "to run," "to build," "to eat."

Jargon The language that only someone in a particular trade, profession or group would ordinarily know: medical jargon, legal jargon, educational jargon, computer jargon.

Nouns The names of people, places and things: Bob, New York, ball.

Passive voice Passive voice is when some action is being done to the subject of a sentence: "The ball was hit by John." "Ball" is the subject; the action is being done to the ball.

Prefix Literally: something that comes before something else. In grammatical constructions: a group of letters that contain meaning and are placed before a root word to form a new word:

prefix "un" + root "kind" = "unkind"
prefix "per" + root "figure" = "prefigure"

Prepositions Words that show the relationship between two other words in a sentence: "Michael Harrington, 35, of 19 High Street, in Birmington, was shot yesterday as he drove over the section of I-65 currently under construction." Some common prepositions are:

above	beside	over
across	by	through
after	except	to
against	for	toward
along	in	under
among	into	until
around	near	up
at	of	upon
before	off	with
behind	on	within
below	outside	without

Suffix Literally: something that follows something else. In grammatical construction: a group of letters containing meaning that are added to the end of a root word to form a new word:

root "kind" + suffix "ly" = kindly
root "strike" + suffix "ing" = striking

Run-ons Too many sentences improperly joined. Sentences must be written separately, or they must be separated by a

semicolon or be joined by a conjunction ("and," "but," "nor").
Examples:

>Run-on: Mike was a poet he was also a critic.
>Correct: Mike was a poet; he was also a critic.

Sentence A complete thought.

Syntax The way words are put together in a phrase or sentence.

Verbs Words that express some kind of action or state of being:

>Action: "John won the contest."
>State: "John is overweight."